THE FEDERAL RESERVE

WHAT EVERYONE NEEDS TO KNOW

THE FEDERAL RESERVE

WHAT EVERYONE NEEDS TO KNOW

STEPHEN H. AXILROD

OXFORD
UNIVERSITY PRESS

OXFORD

UNIVERSITY PRESS

Oxford University Press is a department of the University of Oxford.
It furthers the University's objective of excellence in research, scholarship,
and education by publishing worldwide.

Oxford   New York
Auckland   Cape Town   Dar es Salaam   Hong Kong   Karachi
Kuala Lumpur   Madrid   Melbourne   Mexico City   Nairobi
New Delhi   Shanghai   Taipei   Toronto

With offices in
Argentina   Austria   Brazil   Chile   Czech Republic   France   Greece
Guatemala   Hungary   Italy   Japan   Poland   Portugal   Singapore
South Korea   Switzerland   Thailand   Turkey   Ukraine   Vietnam

Oxford is a registered trademark of Oxford University Press
in the UK and certain other countries.

Published in the United States of America by Oxford University Press
198 Madison Avenue, New York, NY 10016

Library of Congress Cataloging-in-Publication Data
Axilrod, S. H.
The Federal Reserve : what everyone needs to know / Stephen H. Axilrod.
pages cm
ISBN 978–0–19–993448–5 (hardcover : alk. paper)—ISBN 978–0–19–993447–8
(pbk. : alk. paper)—ISBN (invalid) 978–0–19–993449–2 (updf)
1. Board of Governors of the Federal Reserve System (U.S.)
2. Federal Reserve banks.   3. Monetary policy—United States.
4. United States—Economic policy.
I. Title.
HG2563.A95 2013
332.1'10973—dc23
2012046769

CONTENTS

3 Basic Monetary Policy Objectives 28

4 Instruments of Monetary Policy 41

5 The Formulation and Communication of Monetary Policy   64

8 Conclusion 127

PREFACE

This book aims to clarify for a broad public audience what the Federal Reserve System, the nation's central bank, does, while still being of interest to former colleagues and others who study and evaluate its practices. It emphasizes the institution's principal function of monetary policy, including closely related financial and regulatory issues, and answers questions about what are its capabilities and limitations and why it does what it does.

A central bank is an entity with singularly enormous powers to influence financial markets and the economy, given to it by the nation through the legislative process. Historically, the Federal Reserve's workings have been little understood by the public. However, in recent decades—featuring worries about too much inflation, fears of deflation, and most recently the debilitating aftermath of what appears to have been the granddaddy of all credit crises—it has become much more widely discussed in the media, often abused and occasionally praised.

It has been dragged into the open air where, indeed, it long ought to have been. In those circumstances, the Federal Reserve has become more and more forthcoming about its intentions, motivations, actual policy decisions made, and future prospects.

This writer has experienced the Federal Reserve and how its policies have been formulated in the post–World War II period from both a first-hand, inside perspective and an outside perspective not far from the line of fire. First, almost three and a half decades were spent on the inside, much of the time working closely on policy with the chairmen of the period. Subsequently, more than two active decades have been spent closely observing the Fed from an outside market perspective, for some years as a high official of a foreign (Japanese) securities firm on Wall Street, and then as an independent market consultant both in the United States and abroad (the latter mainly as a consultant to foreign central banks in countries making the transition to a more modern operating framework). These inside and outside views in retrospect seem to have, to use an analogy, leavened the bread with a mixture (sweet, sour, and in between) that should improve its texture, though taste may always be in dispute.

My views about the Fed and thoughts about "what everyone needs to know"—the writ offered by the Oxford University Press—were influenced not only by firsthand and close continuing observations of the institution's doings but also by the many fascinating and knowledgeable people I met along the way. The list would be far too long to individualize and includes not only central bank officials here and abroad (many of whom were economists) but also academic thinkers on the subject, market participants struggling to understand what the institution was up to, envoys of the political world who might have the same problem, and others—like friends and neighbors—who ask questions, some with puzzled looks.

With respect to this particular book, I would like to give thanks to Ed Nelson, a widely experienced monetary and macro-economist, currently an assistant director in the Division of Monetary Affairs at the Board of Governors of the Federal Reserve System. He read through an early draft of the text and provided a number of specific and helpful technical comments.

All remaining errors are my responsibility, and so, of course, are all opinions and interpretations.

I would also like to recognize, with love, my wife, Kathy, who withstood her husband's ups and downs as he tried to figure out not only what the public needs to know, but also how to clarify in his own mind the complex, continually evolving issues for policy and the Federal Reserve that have been unveiled by the great credit crisis and its difficult aftermath.

1
INTRODUCTION

Why is the Federal Reserve (the Fed) so important to the country?

The Fed is the nation's central bank and, as authorized by law, independently determines the country's monetary policy. It has a unique capacity to control inflation, helps moderate cyclical ups and downs in the economy, and acts as a buffer against potentially destabilizing financial and credit market conditions. Policy is normally implemented mainly through three traditional policy instruments: open market operations in government securities, lending via its discount window, and setting reserve requirements on bank deposits.

The Fed also has an important role in establishing the nation's regulatory policies in the financial area, especially as they apply to commercial banks and certain related entities. Such policies can impinge on and interact with monetary policy and the use of monetary instruments. While a central bank's monetary policy function is special, its regulatory role is similar to, and shared with, other regulatory authorities in the country. Many, but not all, central banks around the world combine both monetary policy and a certain regulatory authority.

When and why was the Fed founded?

The Fed was originally established in December 1913 under very different economic and financial conditions than currently exist in the United States and the rest of the world. At that time, the financial panics and breakdowns in the banking system that had all too frequently unsettled our economy impelled the Congress to create an institution (the Federal Reserve System) with lending, regulatory, and other powers that could, it was thought, moderate, if not avert, significant financial disruptions.

How did the Fed evolve?

The original Federal Reserve Act was subsequently modified a number of times. As experience was gained with the central bank's basic monetary policy instruments, their unique influence on the nation's overall credit and money conditions became better understood. At the same time, the United States developed into a major worldwide financial and economic power, with increasingly dynamic, and unfortunately still occasionally crisis-prone, markets; the stock market crisis of 1929, the banking crisis of the early 1930s, and the credit crisis of 2008–2009 were among the most notable. Practical experience and ongoing economic research helped guide legislative changes that affected the economic and financial role of the Fed and its monetary policy objectives, but not without considerable and occasionally acrimonious debate.

Monetary policy came to be clearly recognized as one of the two major so-called macro-economic tools, along with the U.S. government's fiscal policy, which help to assure that everyone who wants a job can get one and that the average level of prices remains generally stable. Like other central banks around the world, the Fed is especially concerned with maintaining reasonable price stability over time. In the course of the great inflation of the 1970s, the public became increasingly aware of the institution's responsibilities to contain inflation. But it also makes decisions to help keep economic activity on an even keel and to avert dangerous financial instabilities—issues that brought the Fed under enormous public and political scrutiny as the great credit crisis of 2008–2009 and its aftermath unfolded.

The Fed will celebrate its 100th anniversary in 2013. The Fed of today came into its own after amendments to the Federal Reserve Act by the mid-1930s improved, among other things, the organizational basis for policy, and after 1951, when the institution was freed from agreed restraints that helped finance the Second World War at low interest rates. This book will draw mainly on the experiences of the post–World War II years in its discussion of the monetary policy structure and operation of the institution, along with regulatory issues that have been so prominently raised in recent years in connection with the Fed and monetary policy.

How in general does the Fed compare with other central banks?

Central banks are a familiar species in our modern world. They come in all shapes and sizes, and are freighted with varying responsibilities and degrees of independence from the central government.

Central banks have been prevalent and important to economic and financial policy in the developed world for a long time. In recent decades, as political conditions and economic philosophies have changed around the world, central banks in emerging and less developed countries have begun to evolve, quite slowly in many instances, toward modern-style central banks with powers more typical of those in the developed world. How advanced or not a central bank may be, and while differing in a number of important respects, they all tend to feature, in one way or another, the essential central banking power for strongly influencing overall credit and money conditions in the country.

As a central bank, the Fed is akin to diverse institutions among the major economic countries of the world such as the Bank of England (BoE) in the United Kingdom, the European Central Bank (ECB), the Bank of Japan (BoJ) and, although rather more remotely, the Peoples Bank of China (PBC). All except the PBC have a certain amount of basic independence like the Fed and wield their policy instruments in similar ways. In practice, the PBC differs in both respects at the present time. However, the regulatory roles among major central banks differ and seem to be in a state of flux.

The BoE, whose day-to-day monetary operations are rather similar to those of the Fed, has not been spared from the recent spate of financial crises afflicting financially important countries or currency areas. Interestingly enough, the crisis was, as in the United States, attributed in good part to inadequate regulation. The result was to transfer back to the BoE responsibilities that had been transferred out not so long before as a result of political dissatisfaction with an earlier regulatory oversight by the bank. What goes around comes around, so it would seem. The BoE could, and did, of course continue to carry out its monetary policy without regulatory authority, but regulatory authority apparently could not be handled effectively without a key role for the BoE.

The crisis in the United States initially caused a huge adverse political reaction to the Fed's handling of its regulatory responsibilities, including many threats to remove them. In the end, some peripheral ones were removed, but other important ones were added by new fundamental financial legislation passed in 2010.

The ECB, unlike other central banks, is not the bank for a single country with its own overriding political and social system and fiscal authority. Rather, the ECB serves as the sole monetary and currency authority for a large group of countries (17 as of this writing) within the European Union that employ the Euro as their common currency. Regulatory and supervisory responsibilities for banks and other financial institutions are dispersed among the individual countries of both the Euro zone and the EU as a whole. Of course, continuing efforts at coordination are undertaken through various mechanisms within the area, and greater efforts to bring regulation more closely into harmony were set in motion by the intensified Euro credit crisis of very recent years.

Nonetheless, it appears to be the weakness in central political leadership and of fiscal coordination in the Euro zone that has most prominently created the potential for severe economic and market tensions associated with the recent credit crisis, although regulatory decentralization has not been without its problems in that respect. The widely publicized Euro credit crisis of 2011–2012 (which had been festering for some time) was highlighted by unsustainably expansive fiscal (and also in some cases instances private sector) policies in a few countries that generated far too much of a debt burden for them to handle. This in turn threatened the systemic stability and credibility of the Euro banking and market as whole, as the questionable debt was widely held throughout the system.

The PBC, unlike the Fed, is an integral part of the executive branch of the Chinese government; the PBC's fundamental decisions are dependent on higher authorities. It has been slowly modernized—gradually given more powers (such as greater control of loans made by its regional offices) to make it more effective in implementing a national monetary policy. But because of the lack of breadth and depth in Chinese banking and financial markets, the PBC so far relies mostly on reserve requirement changes at banks and terms and conditions at its discount windows to signal policy shifts toward tightening or easing, rather than open market operations.

Many other countries have made efforts to modernize their central banks in recent decades. In Eastern Europe, some had originally been established in highly controlled economies (such as the USSR) and had been in business merely to dispense loan funds when and where needed to meet some national economic plan. With the fall of communism, the central banks in Russia and the former satellite countries were refitted by the newly established regimes with monetary instruments geared to influencing overall credit market conditions and economic activity and prices. Generally, however, they would seem to be without a significant capability for establishing monetary policies based on their own best judgments.

Around our rapidly integrating economic and financial world, central banks, such as those in the Middle East and North Africa, are attempting to find their way to more active and constructive roles in countries that are looking toward stable growth and financial stability in an increasingly interactive and competitive global economic environment.

How does a central bank differ from other banks and financial institutions?

As a basis for monetary policy, all central banks have certain features in common that, unlike individual commercial banks and other depository and financial institutions, give them the potential for unrivaled and enormous influence in financial markets and the economy. For one, they are, as the bankers' bank, the ultimate source of loans to commercial banks and certain other depositories; they hold working balances (including required reserves, if any) behind deposits for the institutions and provide clearing and payments services. For another, the central banks' writ from the government permits them to acquire other assets, mainly government and government-guaranteed securities and to a certain extent other types of securities. These two features mean that central banks in effect have the power to create money, liquidity, and credit out of thin air.

It happens, illustratively, this way. To get the funds for assets it buys or for loans that it may make, a central bank, unlike ordinary businesses, does not have to draw down any of its existing assets, borrow or raise equity from another entity or the public, or divert income. The central bank pays by simply crediting the reserve balance accounts it holds for member banks for the asset or loan it takes on.

Since any individual commercial bank normally needs to hold only some fraction (often quite small) of its deposits as reserves at the central bank for operating and legal purposes, the reserve balances are quickly spread throughout the banking system (aided by the efficient interbank federal funds market in the United States). They provide the base for a rather rapid, multiple expansion in bank credit and deposits that also affects, through customer linkages, financial markets and interest rates more broadly throughout the economy.

How do the Fed's unique policy instruments affect the nation's economy as a whole?

In response to the emerging interest rate effects and changes in credit availability and liquidity from the Fed's actions, the nation's economic well-being will be eventually affected in one way or another—indicated by the behavior of economic activity, employment, and the average level of prices. In practice, it takes some time for those influences to be felt. Moreover, the Fed's degree of influence is not easy to distinguish, given all the other influences, both domestic and international, that weigh on the economy. Over the long run, however, a central bank with its power to create money out of nothing, so to speak, does bear a clear, special responsibility for the behavior of inflation.

A central bank's powers to create credit or money, in addition to being crucial to its monetary policy function, also serve as a buffer against destabilizing and economically disruptive financial crises. The recent credit crises in the United States and subsequently in Europe, for instance, were contained, at least to a degree, through an unusually large expansion in the balance sheet of central banks as they provided funds to markets that were being dragged down by bad debts.

In general, the Fed and other central banks can be viewed as unique institutions that, in their money- and credit-creating powers, have the power independently, from on high as it were, to tilt the ongoing balance of supply and demand in financial markets. They are something like the proverbial deus ex machina that usefully appears in a literary work from out of nowhere and transforms its plot. However, central banks cannot control the ensuing plot development like an author can, and the eventual outcomes of their intervention are shrouded in uncertainty even if the direction appears clear. That, by the way, is essentially why good central banking depends so much on sound judgment and an almost intuitive feel for markets by its leadership as much as, or more than, practically useful results of economic analysis and research.

If so crucial to national policy, why is the Fed independent of the government?

Central banks that are considered independent, such as the Fed, are essentially independent within the government, but, they are by no means independent of the government. In the United States, for example, the Fed's powers are granted by Congress and can be altered by that body (and, of course, are subject to presidential veto and judicial review). The practical test of a central bank's monetary policy independence is the extent to which it can determine its monetary policy stance and make operating decisions without approval by the executive branch of the government.

It is the enormous powers inherent in the structure of a central bank that both entice governments to maintain direct control over the bank through its executive branch and also provide incentives to give its central bank a certain degree of independence. At this point in time, central banks in developed, democratic countries have in fact been given a significant degree of independence in decision-making about monetary policy and its implementation.

Partly, this has been to help ensure that the powers of the central bank are not used to doctor markets during election periods to favor the incumbent party. But importantly, over the past several decades, it has reflected growing recognition that it is in everyone's interest to keep inflation in check over time and that the central bank, as the institution with unique powers to do so, should be distanced from politics so it can more readily focus on its principal task of keeping inflation down by controlling the nation's monetary base.

Early in the post–World War II period, a then long-serving chairman of the Fed, William McChesney Martin, took to describing the Fed as independent within the government (a phrase that he probably did not originate). He also became well-known for aptly describing the Fed's principal problem by noting that it was the institution's (unhappy) job to take the punch bowl away once the party really got going.

But when exactly is that? The art of central banking is largely in the timing, plus a feel for how markets might respond under circumstances of the period—not easy to get right, given all the conflicting signals and tendencies in an economy, in its markets, and in its connections to the rest of the world.

2

THE FED'S ORGANIZATION FOR POLICY

Where does responsibility for monetary policy decisions reside in the Fed?

Though organized as a regional system, with 12 Federal Reserve Banks around the country, monetary policy and other major decisions are made on a national basis. The dominant role is played by the seven-person politically appointed Board of Governors of the Federal Reserve System located in Washington, DC. The Board also oversees operations of the Reserve Banks and approves key decisions such as who will be named presidents of them.

As to monetary policy, Board members are the majority of the 12-member Federal Open Market Committee (FOMC), the central monetary policymaking body within the Fed. It was established by law in early amendments to the Act, attaining its present form in 1942. In addition to seven Board members, the committee includes the president of the Federal Reserve Bank of New York and four of the 11 other regional Reserve Bank presidents serving in annual rotations. The nonvoting presidents also sit at the table at each meeting and participate fully in policy discussions.

What does the FOMC do and how is it organized?

The FOMC is the key organization within the Fed responsible for monetary policy. It has control over the purchase and sale of securities in the market, and also foreign exchange operations. It sets the guidelines for day-to-day securities transactions in the market and thereby controls the federal funds rate, or whatever other operating objectives the Committee may adopt; these transactions in turn influence the Fed's balance sheet and the nation's monetary base, as noted in the preceding chapter.

By law, the FOMC organizes itself. Neither its chairman nor vice chairman is designated in the law. While its membership changes annually, every year, by tradition, the members elect the sitting chairman of the Board of Governors to be chairman of the Committee; similarly, the president of the New York Fed is annually chosen to be vice chairman. When attending the meetings as a staff person, I always sensed the slightest tremor of the unthinkable around the table when the motion was brought to a vote (a young man's imagination most likely).

The key economic, legal, and secretariat staff officials who serve the Committee are annually nominated by the chairman from the top staff of the Board, with one exception. The exception is a senior official of the New York Fed, who is responsible for implementing policy decisions in the market. The Board's staff also produces the basic economic projections and policy alternatives—well-known, respectively, as the green book and the blue book—made available in advance to the FOMC as background for its deliberations. It is not so strange that Reserve Bank officials can sometimes come to feel that the Board looms a bit too large over the proceedings.

How are other monetary policy instruments controlled?

Monetary policy can also be implemented through two other instruments often referred to in textbooks and employed in practice to varying degrees: reserve requirements (set for banks and certain other depository institutions), and the discount window (shorthand for the terms and conditions of loans made by Reserve Banks). Reserve requirements are fully under the control of the Board of Governors, but they are seldom changed these days in the United States or in other countries with well-developed, broad markets, where banks face strong domestic and international competition for business. Certain other instruments, subject directly to control of the Board, have been added to the Fed's arsenal in recent years in the wake of the credit crisis.

Terms under which banks and other eligible institutions may borrow from Reserve Banks are also within the Board's control. Under the Federal Reserve Act, the Boards of Directors of regional Reserve Banks forward discount rate recommendations to the Board in Washington on a regular basis. The Board in Washington then votes to confirm, deny, or table the recommendation in the context of its broad legal power to "review and determine" the rate. While the ultimate power held by the Board is clear, it is practically awkward to determine a rate in the absence of a recommendation from a Reserve Bank. In that sense, incoming discount rate recommendations from Reserve Bank boards provide a useful, and occasionally influential, indicator of sentiment about economic developments around the country and the potential direction of monetary policy.

Through regulations that it issues the Board also governs other lending conditions at the discount window, such as the minimum bank examination rating needed for regular credit access. Finally, beginning in 2002, the Board overhauled its discount window regulations, in practice easing access to the discount window by banks in good standing. At the same time, the basic discount rate (now technically termed the "primary credit rate") was, by regulation, to be set at a penalty to the federal funds rate targeted by the FOMC.

How is the politically appointed Board of Governors chosen?

The seven governors on the Board are the only political appointees in the Fed. The president of the United States nominates them, presumably from among candidates with whom he feels comfortable, and they are subject to confirmation by the Senate. Governors are limited to one 14-year term, the length reinforcing, one would suppose, the Fed's independence. From my observations, it is somewhat unusual for a governor to serve a full term; for many, it seems to be something of a stepping-stone.

No more than one governor is supposed to come from a single Federal Reserve district, and due consideration is to be given to the geographic and occupational distribution of the nominees. These considerations have been interpreted quite liberally in modern times owing to the evolution of very fluid national markets, labor and business mobility, and economic and price conditions that for the most part have become national in scope—although regional economic differences do, of course, persist. A developing perception that central banking is something of an arcane technical profession has led to the increasing representation of economists, albeit with varying backgrounds, on the Board (as well as presidents of Reserve Banks).

On the other hand, legislative standards can also be interpreted quite strictly when politically suitable, as in very recent years when strong ideological and strategic disagreements in Congress delayed and forestalled nominees for governors. One result was a sustained period when the Board consisted of no more than five governors, thus unfortunately diluting needed leadership at the Fed during the pressure-packed credit crisis episode.

One of the governors is nominated as chairman for a four-year term; another as vice chairman for a term of equal length; and a third, as required by an amendment in 2010, is also designated vice chairman for Supervision for a four-year term (who is still not appointed as of this writing, although the function can be undertaken by any governor designated by the chairman).

The amendment creating the supervision vice chairman was contained in the very lengthy and perhaps overly complex Dodd-Frank Wall Street Reform and Consumer Protection Act (DFA) passed in July 2010 by Congress in response to the credit crisis and dissatisfaction with the Fed's (and other institutions') regulatory and supervisory performance leading up to it. The Act included a number of provisions affecting the Fed—a few relatively minor governance changes and also other more substantive ones affecting regulatory responsibilities and use of the discount window especially for special emergency purposes.

How are Reserve Banks governed?

Each regional Reserve Bank is governed by a nine-person Board of Directors, which appoints a president to be CEO, subject to approval by the Board of Governors. By law, the Reserve Bank Board is composed of three so-called Class A directors, who represent the stockholding banks (member banks); three Class B directors, none of whom may be employees of a member bank and who represent the public generally, including various aspects of business, labor, and agriculture; and three Class C directors designated by the Board of Governors also to represent the public broadly, one of whom with "tested" banking experience being chosen as chairman.

(A map showing boundaries of the country's 12 Federal Reserve districts and locations of the principal Federal Reserve Banks is displayed in figure 2.1.)

With passage of the DFA, Class A directors can no longer cast a vote for president of a Reserve Bank. This represents a shot across the bow to warn the Fed that Congress remains wary of connections between senior Fed officials and top banking executives—a worry aroused by fears that undue interactions might have occurred in the handling of the credit crisis.

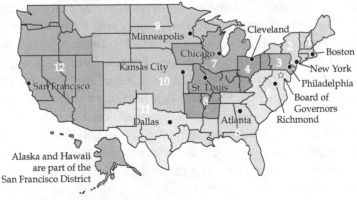

Figure 2.1 Map of the Federal Reserve System
Source: Board of Governors of the Federal Reserve System. www.federalreserve.gov/otherfrb.htm

Approval by the Board of Governors of the directors' nominees for Reserve Bank presidencies is usually a fairly smooth process, although some little contention is not unknown. Often Reserve Bank presidents are appointed from within the bank, but it is not unusual for an outsider to be named.

What role do Reserve Banks play in the policy process?

As noted, the Federal Reserve Banks and their principal officials play an important, though somewhat subsidiary role, in the formation of monetary policy—the most important clearly being the vote by their presidents on the FOMC, followed by the discount rate recommendations made by their boards. However, the Reserve Banks are crucial to implementing the System's policies—monetary policy at the New York Fed and other policies (such as lending, regulatory, and clearing and payments services) at all the regional banks. In addition, and importantly, the 12 Reserve Banks play a key role as the eyes and ears of the Fed around the country.

They enhance, through their role in bank supervision and examination, the Fed's awareness, of developments and also, one would hope, of early signs of attitudinal shifts in banking and by extension related areas of business and finance. In addition, continued contacts—via speeches, informal meetings, and usual business interactions—by the presidents and other staff throughout the banks' Federal Reserve districts usefully can garner a sense of changes in spending habits and psychology at the grassroots level. Such a sense can help judge the significance of the various national surveys with which the country is now almost continuously bombarded. In addition, regional outreach by Reserve Banks helps to increase local understanding of what the Fed is try to accomplish and why.

These regional interactions, along with the Fed's local operating services, help make the Fed part of a community instead of simply a remote uncaring Washington bureaucracy. That is not without certain other advantages; they contribute to a kind of political support that helps sustain the basic institutional credibility needed by the Fed.

The more credible, the more effectively can the Fed work with its congressional overseers and with the executive branch. It will be better able to carry out its monetary policy as it objectively sees fit, even in face of political and public doubts and overt opposition, and to survive independently to fight another day in the event of stumbles. Nonetheless, institutional credibility in practice certainly depends on much more than the Fed's regional activities. It can be seriously dented if the public loses confidence in the institution's ability to contain inflation, as in the 1970s. And it was severely tested and noticeably hurt in the course of the credit crisis.

Should the regional structure of the Fed be modified for today's world?

It is true enough that the existing Fed structure has begun to look a bit outmoded as a result of advances in financial technology as well as marked changes in the structure of banking, including expansion of branch banking across state lines and the evolution of nationwide bank holding companies encompassing a variety of related financial businesses. The system of Reserve Bank districts originally designed still works effectively, but if one conceived of establishing a similar system in today's geographic distribution of business and financial activity rather than that of a century ago, different Reserve district boundaries would have to be considered as would the number of Reserve districts as well as the location of Reserve Banks (and of associated branch banks) within them.

But whether such an approach, with all its practical and political difficulties, is needed under present conditions seems doubtful. Over the years ahead, further technological changes may force an even more cost-effective centralization of certain services within the Fed system. For instance, the often fairly sizeable district economic staffs could show some attrition as the cost-cutting affecting private financial institutions in the wake of the credit crisis becomes reflected in certain parts of the Fed. And the ineluctable advance of technology suggests the potential for greater efficiencies in payments services.

On the other hand, the Fed will probably have to take on and retain more staff in the regulatory and supervisory areas in view of perceived deficiencies that surfaced in the credit crisis period. The new requirement for a governor to be nominated as vice chairman for supervision seems to be an attempt to make the Fed focus more effectively on that area of its work.

On balance, it appears reasonable to leave well enough alone for now insofar as the Fed's regional structure is concerned. It has lasted a very long time in face of far-reaching and unanticipated innovations in banking and finance. And it probably has many more years to go before anything other than adjustments manageable within the existing system would need to be considered.

Should Reserve Bank presidents be politically appointed?

Yet another question affecting Reserve Banks, and one more directly related to monetary policy, is raised from time to time and has received some notice in the backwash of the credit crisis. Because Reserve Bank presidents serve on the FOMC, a question is sometimes raised about whether presidents, since they vote on national monetary policy, should be subject to a political appointment process just as the governors of the Fed. Still, the subject has not been actively pressed in the legislature. It raises a host of knotty issues not deemed worth political battles given the obvious practical domination by the politically appointed Board of Governors of the policymaking process during the postwar years.

The present system seems like a good compromise between two extremes. One would be to turn all heads of Reserve Banks into presidential appointees confirmed by the Senate. That approach, however, risks reducing the expertise and objectivity of Reserve Bank presidents if local political debts begin to take precedence in choosing them. The other extreme would be to remove voting rights at the FOMC from all presidents, though not necessarily attendance and full participation in discussions. That approach too has real disadvantages. That all Reserve Bank presidents have an opportunity to vote on monetary policy enhances the prestige of the position, adds a sense of meaning and importance to Reserve Banks in their areas and by extension to the Fed as an institution throughout the country, and probably raises the quality of candidates for the bank presidencies.

A variant would be to make only the president of the New York Fed subject to governmental nomination and confirmation procedures, which did have recent, apparently serious congressional consideration. But that would do little except seem to enhance the standing and influence of Wall Street and major private financial institutions on the nation's monetary policy relative to other sections of the country.

Do member banks and directors of Federal Reserve Banks unduly profit or exert influence?

It seems to me that neither the member banks of district Reserve Banks nor the individual directors of such Banks are likely to gain monetarily from belonging to the Fed. Indeed, for member banks themselves, the cost of membership has appeared at times to outweigh its benefits. The value of membership in the System is essentially intangible. And its main reward would appear to be the status (and whatever benefit that has for customer relations) from participation in a system designed to help, over time, safeguard the country's banking and financial system.

Member banks are the sole stockholders of Federal Reserve Banks. National banks are required to join the Fed by law, while state banks have the option. Members must, upon joining, acquire stock in the their district Reserve Bank equal to 6% of their paid-in capital and surplus, and in remuneration they receive a fixed return of 6% on their investment. The total contribution would rise over time as a bank's capital and surplus grows, but half of that could be, and usually is, subject to call rather than paid. All in all, the monetary income from belonging to the Fed is essentially small for a bank and does not in and of itself provide any real incentive to join.

There are some benefits, of course. Membership in the Fed itself might be one if it raises public confidence in the bank. Another would be privileged access to the Fed's discount window and the convenience of direct access to the Fed's clearing and payments system. Of course, the evolution of a highly liquid broad national market for interbank loans and the ease of correspondent banking have made Fed membership less and less necessary especially for smaller banks. In any event, whatever the benefits to banks, they have to be weighed against the burden of holding reserve requirements against deposits.

In the early decades of the postwar period, state-chartered institutions became less and less interested in joining the Fed and some national banks, even large ones, shifted to a state charter in order to avoid the reserve requirement cost of being in the System. The growing competition from other institutions such as mutual savings banks, savings and loan associations, credit unions, and eventually money market funds were a continuing inducement for banks to economize on costs to remain competitive not only in domestic markets but, for large banks, also in face of growing competition from abroad.

The upshot of all this was enactment of laws in the early 1980s that made important changes designed to keep the central bank's monetary instruments well integrated with the newly evolving financial world. One of the side effects was to alleviate worries at the Fed about whether declining membership in the central bank would attenuate its policy effectiveness. Whether such worries were reasonable or not, it was true that commercial banks—the Fed's customers so to speak— were becoming less unique in the financial world, certainly as suppliers of credit and even, to an important degree, as holders of balances that represent money or near-monies.

In consequence of the congressionally mandated changes, reserve requirements set by the Fed were to be held not only by member banks but also by nonmember banks and various types of thrift institutions. In return, such depository institutions were given access to the Fed's discount window on the same terms as member banks. As of this writing, reserve requirements are levied at a relatively modest rate only on transactions deposits, mainly demand deposits over a minimum amount; moreover, since the fall of 2008, the Fed is permitted to pay interest on required reserve balances (and also excess reserves). Thus, pecuniary considerations have become virtually irrelevant to membership by a commercial bank in the Fed.

Whether Reserve Bank directors exert undue influence on the Fed's policy decisions (beyond what is involved in simply doing one's appointed job by voting on discount rate recommendations) or realize undue personal financial profits from an ongoing association with the Fed are other matters sometimes raised in connection with the Fed's unique structure. Aside from surprisingly few instances over the decades of what might be termed very small-time corruption, the Fed has seemed remarkably free of anything scandalous. Based on my more than three decades of experience within the Fed (at the Board), one could readily sense that a morally strong culture pervaded the system.

Members of Reserve Bank boards, of course, have access to considerable economic and financial information in the course of their services. But the only thing of real value to insiders would be knowledge of a forthcoming monetary policy decision or an actual decision before announcement. The directors, of course, know their own discount rate recommendations to the Board, though that does not presage the basic monetary policy decision with any certainty, and especially so since the discount window was restructured. In any event, neither the directors nor, for that matter, anyone else in the whole country will know the FOMC's monetary policy decision until it is actually made and, nowadays, announced publicly immediately thereafter.

Indeed, in long ago days, I (then staff director and secretary of the FOMC) often met one-on-one with the chairman of the Fed during late-morning rest breaks from the FOMC meeting. The chairman might want to discuss how the meeting would proceed. Vivid in my memory is one such conversation when neither he nor I had any strong feeling about what the outcome would be. Of course the mystery is much, much less for insiders than outsiders, but some mystery always remains.

Of more practical importance, the possibility of undue influence by financially sophisticated Reserve Bank directors on Fed activities, not usually of much public concern, became more contentious during the recent credit crisis period. In so dangerous and unprecedented a situation, the Fed would naturally seek whatever background knowledge it could get to help make the most practically useful decisions. Moreover, the quite unusual loans made by the Fed in the circumstances were generally under the emergency loan provisions of the Federal Reserve Act, which, in those days, governed loans made to nonmember institutions (those provisions being amended and substantially changed by the DFA). They required not only a five- person vote of the Board of Governors but also approval by the board of the lending Reserve Bank (mainly the New York Fed in those instances) of what was "acceptable collateral" in the situation. Obviously, much conversation about the financial circumstances and stabilizing need for such loans was in order in the process of making the loans.

Be that as it may, the relationships between leaders from the financial community (whether Reserve Bank directors or not) and Fed governors do carry a risk. They could shade over from useful knowledge that aids the Fed in maintaining financial stability to advice unduly, even if unconsciously, guided by self-interest. That, of course, is a potential issue not only at the Fed, but also for central banks around the world. In our very open society, it seems to be a question that is, or has become, well recognized and well understood.

What happens to the profits from Fed operations?

Practically all the large net income (after administrative and other operating expenses) from the Fed's monetary policy and other functions is turned over to the U.S. Treasury in its role as the government's tax collector. These distributions are employed, as are tax receipts in general, to help finance the federal budget.

In 2010 and 2011, these distributions were much higher than usual—running in the $75 to $80 billion range, more than three times larger than distributions in the more normal years of the first decade of the this new century. Payments to the Treasury rose sharply because the Fed expanded its balance sheet and interest-earning assets, mainly U.S. government securities on balance, substantially in the course of the credit crisis and its aftermath. (In a normal period, the Fed's earnings are sustained mostly by the large amount of interest earned on U.S. government securities held as backing against the institution's liability for currency outstanding.)

In that way, a fairly sizeable amount of government debt in the hands of the public was in effect retired. The government pays interest to the Fed, and the Fed in turn returns practically all of it to the government. The amount of interest that has to be paid out of taxes levied on consumers and businesses is commensurately reduced. This looks like something of a good deal because it eases the public's tax burden.

That may seem to be advantageous in an early postcrisis period. However, if the Fed's balance sheet, and thus the nation's monetary base, were to continue to expand further, or even remain so expansive, risks to the nation's economic well-being would rise. The principal risk would come if very low interest rates and excess liquidity encouraged too much inflation and its ubiquitous potentially large tax burden as represented by drains on the real value of money and other market assets and on the real spending power of people's income. That's another illustration of the basic argument for an independent central bank. It should be better able than one under the control of the government to resist temptations to monetize the public debt.

What is the underlying connection between the government and the Fed?

The Fed is a creature of Congress, which has delegated its constitutionally given authority over the nation's money to the institution. In that context, the profits from the Fed's operations paid to the government can be viewed as a modern-day form of "seignorage," a term that describes the return taken in olden times by the lord of the manor for sanctioning the means of exchange used on his lands. He would, for example, chip away at or sweat the gold or other valuable coinage that was distributed. In today's world, the government as a whole is the liege lord, to whom due respect is paid by the central bank in the form of paying over its earnings to keep the relationship in good working order (it is required by law anyhow). The payment by the Fed of virtually all its income to the government is one piece of evidence of the close connection between the nation's central bank and the government.

The connection entails mutual responsibilities. While the Fed returns its profits and, of course, carries out its delegated duties in good faith and with diligence, the government has an implicit obligation to its central bank. The nation, and the rest of the world, expects the government to stand behind the central bank financially, which helps sustain confidence in the country's basically fiat money, issued by and through the Fed, as an acceptable medium of exchange. The Fed and the government are in a fundamental way financially intertwined, a nexus that becomes more evident in crisis periods.

The international value of the dollar held up well during the credit crisis in large part because, in an uncertain time that extended worldwide, investors saw few other reliable currency options. But it also held up at least in some part because there was confidence that the Fed could take unusual balance sheet risks—and probably more and sooner than it had probably expected—to keep the crisis under control. The Fed's risks were essentially the government's because any losses would raise the government's budget deficit.

Similarly, the government also directly took unusual risks, probably riskier ones than the Fed at the time, through capital payments to banks and others to keep the institutions from going under and deepening the crisis. Though representing longer-run investments that could expect to be recouped, they had the immediate effect of increasing the current budget deficit and were more politically damaging in that sense. (For the most part, so far as can be gauged at the time of this writing, the government has indeed recouped much of its investments.) But in principal, there is no budgetary difference between the

Fed's and the government's own crisis operations. The federal budget ultimately bears the burden in both cases. However, the Fed does greatly expand and contort its balance sheet in the process.

Such a government-central bank connection is implicit in all countries. In less developed countries, on occasion, the government may have to bail out its central bank. This happened, for instance, during the Indonesian crisis of the late 1990s, when in the end, the government had no choice but to inject a sizeable amount of new capital into its failed central bank to keep it and the financial markets at least functional.

How does the government keep tabs on the Fed?

In the United States, the legislative branch of government is the principal counterparty of the Fed. The chairmen of the House and Senate Finance Committees, concerned with banking and related matters (they have different specific designations in each chamber), are, so far as I can see, the most important public officials to the Fed. The president of the United States, of course, nominates governors of the Fed Board and its chairman and vice chairmen. But the Congress remains very sensitive to any indication that the president may attempt to exert any influence on the Fed's domestic policy decisions; especially so, when different political parties control the executive and legislative branches and elections are in sight, as they always seem to be these days.

Congressional oversight through reports and testimony, some on a regular basis and others on demand as problems arise, to relevant committees of the House and Senate are a continuing form of governmental oversight. Regarding monetary policy, the Fed Board makes well-publicized detailed reports semiannually to both the Senate and the House committees that cover banking. These reports are accompanied by testimony from the chairman on behalf of the Board and the FOMC, which consists of long question-and-answer sessions.

The Fed's operations are also subject to audit by the General Accountability Office (GAO), an arm of Congress. However, the monetary policy function—which these days is virtually made in the open and amply reported to the Congress and the public—has not been subject to such audits. But what is policy and what is not are subjects of some tension. Because of serious public questions raised by the Fed's unprecedented lending activities during the worst of the credit crisis, GAO audits were undertaken of those operations and thus have, so it would appear, come to tread on ground a little closer to monetary policy.

Notably of course, Congress retains the power of the purse. Thus far, the Fed's budget is not subject to congressional approval. But the threat that it could be remains real. It is reported in the federal budget. And the possibility of bringing it under the appropriation process encourages great watchfulness at the Board to ensure that not even Caesar's wife could be more pure.

What does it mean in practice to say that the Fed is independent?

Obviously, it does not mean that the Fed is independent of the government, as noted earlier. To reiterate, it is independent within the government, and its areas of independence are indicated or implicit in the Federal Reserve Act.

Its monetary policy operating decisions do not involve approval by any entity within the executive branch of the government up to and including the president. The ultimate objectives of the decisions are, however, stipulated in the Federal Reserve Act. In its modern-day version, the Act (in Section 2A) now specifies the Fed's monetary policy objectives. They are maintenance of long-term growth in monetary and credit aggregates to achieve "maximum employment, stable prices, and moderate long-term interests." These goals govern the independent decisions made by the Board of Governors and the FOMC about monetary policy and its implementation.

There are other powers available to the Fed that are at least tangential to success in achieving monetary policy objectives, but for which it does not have either sole or ultimate control. One has to do with foreign exchange market operations. The other, and more important to financial market stability and the Fed's ability to employ its monetary policy instruments most effectively, involves its regulatory and supervisory responsibilities.

With regard to foreign exchange market operations, control in practice has been in the hands of the U.S. Treasury, whose secretary is considered to be the nation's chief financial officer. Nonetheless, the Fed's own operations in that market require approval by the FOMC. The Fed in that way has an important influence on U.S. exchange market policy, but the Treasury in practice has had ultimate control over the size of operations, if any, whether for the Fed's own account or the Treasury's account (for which the Fed acts as fiscal agent).

With regard to regulatory policy, the Fed may have more independence in action than it does in the foreign exchange market, but by no means does it have the same independence as in monetary policy and instruments directly related to it. At the same time, the Fed implicitly has responsibility for ensuring the underlying stability of financial markets, obviously a goal desirable in and of itself, but also a much-needed objective to support the effectiveness of monetary policy, as the credit crisis and its damaging effect on the economy and market functioning made clear. That responsibility will continue, so it would appear, to require coordination with other regulatory authorities and agencies as modified by the DFA.

3

BASIC MONETARY POLICY OBJECTIVES

What are the Fed's basic objectives?

As noted in the preceding chapter, the goals set for monetary policy in the Federal Reserve Act are maximum employment, stable prices, and low, long-term interest rates. The Fed's other very important objective, the maintenance of systemic stability in financial markets, is left implicit in the powers given to it as lender of last resort and in market regulation. Financial stability has obviously risen considerably in importance since the credit crisis and its aftermath—a severe recession and lingering economic weakness have demonstrated its intimate connection with the Fed's employment objective.

Of the explicit economic objectives set for monetary policy, employment and price goals are clearly dominant. Long-term interest rates appear to have been given such a prominent position by the Congress mainly for political rather than economic purposes. Quite possibly the legislators wished to show special concern for the housing market (with measures to support home ownership, long a congressional vote-getting favorite) or possibly to wave a flag of concern about the need to keep the federal debt burden down (about which tax and spending votes are clearly the heart of the matter but politically contentious). In any event, if the employment and price objectives are attained, long-term interest rates will in the end be low enough and of little public concern.

How does the Fed take account of its long-run economic goals?

By all accounts, the Fed gives equal weight to its legally mandated employment and price objectives in framing monetary policies. In press releases and speeches about policy during recent years, the FOMC and its high officials have quite often referred to them as a "dual mandate" or used other words that represent variations on the same theme. For instance, in early 2012, with economic recovery after the credit crisis still slow, a policy release indicated a particular action taken would be regularly reviewed and adjusted as needed "to promote a stronger economic recovery in a context of price stability."

But in practice, of course, the degree of emphasis given to employment and price objectives in policy implementation naturally varies with economic circumstances. In times of economic recession, employment worries are of paramount importance, and the FOMC will try to lower interest rates until recovery takes hold. Inflation will normally be too low to be of concern most of that time. When recovery advances far enough, inflation tends to show signs of life, and the dual mandate will come into full practical effect.

When inflation is running too high, the price stability part of the mandate will take greater precedence and employment will be of less concern. Then when Fed policies have brought inflation under control, employment questions will become more important, and the mandate will again become operationally dual.

But, for one reason or another, the world always turns out to be more complicated than suggested by such a schematic explanation. Policy does not normally unfold in a smooth and predictable pattern. Monetary policymakers, like anyone else, can have recognition problems about the dynamics driving economic activity under particular circumstances, so the timing and intensity of policy changes are not always as perfect as one might wish—especially when judged in light of that most wonderful benefit hindsight grants to observers and analysts. Or the Fed can be unexpectedly thrown out of its comfort zone by the timing, size, and vast ramifications of one-time economic shocks, like the oil price crises in the 1970s or the equity and credit crises in the early part of the current century, and decision-making becomes less crisp and sure.

Also, at times, surrounding social and broadly political circumstances may impinge more (or less) than usual on the Fed's policy stance in attempting to balance its two main economic objectives. They are not explicit in the course of policy discussions, or perhaps even consciously felt by participants. But it seems, at least to me, that society's tolerance for pushing policy in one direction or another at the risk of incurring either too little employment or too much inflation is something of a background factor in the decision process, and naturally closer to the fore the more difficult are economic and financial conditions.

What role does the Fed chairman play in focusing the institution's economic goals?

While to a degree, hedged in by the economic and sociopolitical environment in which it functions, the Fed is not completely without room to maneuver. How boldly it dares to act will depend for the most part on the personal characteristics of the chairman of the Fed's Board of Governors. He (thus far only men have held the position) is the Fed's undoubted leader in the modern age, although not all chairmen have convincingly fulfilled that role in the eyes of history or of the public. In practice, he alone has the national bully pulpit and internal organizational position that yield a real opportunity to push for significant attitudinal shifts about policy in the mindset of Fed policymakers and concurrently the public.

Chairman Volcker had the vision and bureaucratic nerve to do just that to control inflation in the 1980s. Chairman Burns kept inflation in the 1970s from getting even further out of hand, but he had too cautious an attitude toward policy and toward his own public posture to make active efforts to reduce inflation in the difficult economic and financial circumstances of his time. Chairman Greenspan, as his long and, for a time, quite successful tenure continued, lost sight of, or did not seem to fully grasp, how asset bubbles and regulatory issues could seriously undermine the ability of monetary policy to keep the economy on an even keel.

As it turned out, asset bubbles and continuing regulatory deficiencies held dangers similar to those that inhere in too much inflation. They create excesses that can generate serious recession. And, as they cumulated through the early phase of Chairman Bernanke's tenure, in the end they contributed to a perfect storm out of which a highly threatening credit crisis erupted, followed by a very severe economic downturn and quite slow upturn.

In what sense are the Fed's monetary policy objectives compatible with each other?

As noted, the Fed's objectives of maximum employment and stable prices often conflict with each other in the short- and intermediate-runs. When the conflict is on the extreme side, the Fed must shift its attention more or less entirely from one to the other. However, the first half of Greenspan's lengthy tenure of almost 18 years was a period when the dual mandate appears to have been well satisfied. The early postwar years until about the mid-1960s were, on balance, another. Of course, the periods of high inflation in the 1970s and of asset bubbles and regulatory fecklessness in the opening decade of twenty-first century were times when it was not.

More generally, throughout the post–World War II era, whether in periods when the dual mandate was reasonably in balance or out of kilter, economic activity in the United States, as well as in practically all other countries of the world, has been subject to inherent fluctuations that occur periodically though not very predictably. In response to internal dynamics and associated imbalances of one sort or another that naturally arise, an economy sometimes grows faster in the short-run than in the long-run, and sometimes grows slower or even declines.

These fluctuations, termed business cycles when intense enough, can occur for a number of reasons. For instance, often inventories of goods get out of balance with ongoing sales; consequently, production adjustments need to be made that drag down employment. This was a somewhat more common source of economic cycles in earlier decades before the high-tech revolution made it easier for businesses to better synchronize production with orders and sales.

As another example, investments in long-lasting capital goods, including housing, may be overdone through an excess of business or personal optimism relative to the underlying demand for the goods and services (including for shelter) that the investments produce. An overinvestment in capital goods may well require substantial readjustments—sometimes more intense than in the old-fashioned inventory cycle—that often lead to a period of declining economic activity and employment opportunities, then followed by a recovery as the economy restructures itself.

In general, the mutual compatibility of the Fed's two principal legislated economic objectives, as well as the institution's success in simultaneously achieving them, can be judged not in the short- or, at times, even intermediate-run but only in the long run. To be sure, it is the business of monetary policy— along with, one would hope, a supportive fiscal policy—to help even out the shorter-run fluctuations and cycles of real economic activity. But over a longer span of time, it is really only the price stability objective that is under the control of the Fed. That's because the behavior of prices in the aggregate is essentially a monetary phenomenon—as in "too much money chasing too few goods." Thus, the Fed, because it alone has the ability to control the supply of the nation's monetary base, can be held responsible for inflation in the average level of prices.

However, the Fed's other principal objective, maximum employment, depends over the longer run on real supply side factors that are not under its control. The trend rate of the country's real growth depends basically on birth rates and immigration policies that affect expansion in the nation's labor force, as well as on the myriad of technological innovations and organizational efficiencies that influence its productivity. For example, if productivity were to rise by around 2.25% on average and the labor force by 1.75%, the nation's real output of goods and services would grow on average around 4% over the long run. That will determine the maximum level of employment that evolves over time.

Whether such a level of employment is consistent with an unemployment rate at around, say, 4% (or whatever rate turns out essentially to represent frictional unemployment) depends on, among other things, the characteristics of a country's labor market. Unemployment will be lower and maximum employment higher the more flexible and adaptable the labor market (in terms of, e.g., labor mobility and wage flexibility) and the nation's education and training capacities. They will need to be attuned to shifts in the nation's economic structure that are compelled by continuing innovations, a persistent drive for efficiencies, changing consumer tastes, and ever-more intense competition, as well as opportunities, from developments abroad as the process of internationalization continues and quite possibly accelerates.

In such a complex set of circumstances, one can reasonably say that the Fed has succeeded in meeting its dual mandate if over time it has done what it can to moderate fluctuations or cyclical volatility in economic activity while over the longer run holding inflation within a range that is consistent with price stability.

What does price stability mean?

But what inflation rate on average is indeed consistent with price stability? This has never been an easy question to answer. The simplest response would be to say, "Zero."

That would mean that the average level of all prices in the country does not tend to change over time. There would be ups and downs on average and, of course, trend changes in individual prices in response to shifting tastes, inventions of new products, and other factors. But the average level of all prices would be generally invariant, though it too would unavoidably be subject to some cyclical and other temporary variations.

Nonetheless, the world has seldom witnessed such price behavior. Inflations of varying degrees of intensity have been a common bane. Even deflations have at times been with us, usually at times of excessive economic weakness. But long-sustained periods of overall price stability, featuring little or no change in the average level of prices, have been rare.

Moreover, the Fed in recent years appears to have explicitly rejected zero inflation as a desirable interpretation of price stability. It has not done so, it seems, because of historical evidence suggesting it may not be attainable. Rather, it has done so on operational grounds that zero inflation (attainable or not) would unduly limit the effectiveness of monetary policy in achieving the institution's dual mandate.

What makes the Fed prefer a little rather than no inflation as its practical goal?

The Fed has stressed that if inflation were zero, its scope for fighting against economic weakness by easing monetary policy may be unduly constrained. While an explanation may involve more detail than "what everyone needs to know," it will at least reveal some information helpful in judging the Fed's performance over time in carrying out its monetary policy duties.

The Fed's chief means for easing monetary policy, as persistently noted in this book, is to do what it can to lower market interest rates and ease associated credit and liquidity conditions. Taking the federal funds rate as its usual operating target, the Fed reduced the rate to near zero in the recent crisis, as low as interest rates can go in the market, and has kept it there for a number of years. (Negative market interest rates can pop-up on rare occasions around the world, such as those posted some years ago for deposits by certain Swiss banks and happily paid by wealthy depositors to ensure safety and secrecy.)

While the Fed's market operations of course influence nominal interest rates, a better sense of how easy or tight policy has become is given by a measure of the rate in real terms—that is, by the market federal funds rate less the rate of inflation. For instance, if inflation is to be restrained, the funds rate in the market normally should be above the nation's inflation rate. The real funds rate will thereby be positive, and the higher the better for exerting restraint on inflation. On the other hand, if the economy is weak and inflation is no real problem, the real funds rate would need to be relatively low. It would drop in nominal terms as inflation fell back and credit demand weakened when the economy went through a bad patch.

In a very weak economy, however, the real funds might need to be negative for conventional monetary policy to be as productive as possible. But so long as the average level of prices is essentially unchanged on balance, the real funds rate could never become persistently negative, as it has from time to time in the postwar period. The real funds rate could never fall below the effective zero bound for the market funds rate. (By contrast, to give an example, if inflation were 2%, a zero nominal funds rate would represent a negative 2% real rate, which would have a more expansionary impact on the economy.) Worse yet, in a very depressed economy, if the average level of prices actually slips below zero and declines for a while, the Fed's traditional monetary policy becomes largely counterproductive because the resulting rise in the real funds rate does not portend any positive real benefit in a weakening real economy.

Over the postwar years of positive inflation, the Fed's policies contributed to wide swings in the real funds rate, though not always for the best. Sometimes the rates became negative for too long. One instance occurred during the 1970s high-inflationary period when the nominal market cost of fed funds for several years ran below the rate of inflation in the country. Crudely put, the Fed seemed to be giving away overnight money in real terms when it should have been exerting more restraint on its avail-ability to help suppress inflation. And during the late Greenspan years, following the stock market crash and recession early in the new century, the Fed's subsequent monetary stimulus entailed a few straight years of negative real funds rates—a useful stimulus for a while but probably taken too far as the economy strength-ened and seeds of a credit crisis were taking root.

In the recent credit crisis period, the funds rate in the market was steadily in the area of zero (the actual physical cost of the transaction itself adds just a bit) since the depths of the crisis in late 2008 and during the first three and a half years of the ensu-ing sluggish recovery period (from around mid-2009 through 2012). The inflation rate also hovered near zero, occasionally a little lower and sometimes somewhat higher through most of 2009. Subsequently, however, inflation picked up some and for the past three years the real funds rate has been modestly negative on average.

But that was by no means sufficient to overcome the vast restraining forces, domestic and worldwide, holding back our economic recovery. With the nominal funds rate having reached its practical lower limit, the Fed necessarily, and rather promptly, was forced to expand the nation's monetary base by purchasing longer-term securities to help keep the econ-omy moving forward by providing additional liquidity and attempting to lower other, longer-term interest rates.

Early in the recovery period, a number of economic analysts wanted the Fed to make clear that it would not stand in the way of a (presumably modest) rise in inflation, partly because it would permit a negative real cost for overnight money and maybe help spur the economy forward. Thus far in the recovery period the Fed has evidently not resisted such a rise of inflation. The difference between true price stability and a 1% rise in inflation hardly seems earth shattering, but another percentage point or two would seem to yield a little more real flexibility for conventional monetary policy.

What inflation rate seems to satisfy the goal of price stability?

But apart from operational difficulties for monetary policy, there may also be other much less technical reasons for preferring at least some to no inflation—taking the liberty, as most central banks do, of interpreting its price goal in the broad sense of "reasonable" price stability. At least to this observer, experience in the postwar period seems to show that our economy hums along better and prices also seem reasonably stable to the public when they rise at a quite modest pace, along with a commensurate modest increases in wages.

But if wages and other costs together outpace prices, inflationary pressures tend to intensify as businesses bump up prices of their products in an attempt to maintain profits. If prices then in turn outpace costs, the real income of workers would drop to the detriment of the economy and social stability. The country would be in danger of experiencing an old-fashioned dynamic whereby costs and prices push each other up and up as each sector seeks to compensate for earlier real losses. It would become more difficult in those circumstances to keep inflation expectations from rising and becoming a disruptive factor in economic and market decision-making. The Fed's job would become much harder.

In practice, I judge that low inflation is much less likely than high inflation to give rise to a tendency for inflation to accelerate unacceptably and disruptively. Moreover, while the evidence is not totally clear, it does seem that low rates of inflation do not impair real economic growth, but that higher rates are more likely to do so.

Based in part on experience during the more stable parts of the postwar years and of other countries with similar economic and financial structures as the United States, a low rate of inflation that may well be generally sustainable (in relatively normal times) without raising problems over the longer run for implementation of the dual mandate might be fairly represented as a 1.5% to 3% annual rate range, give or take a little.

Has the Fed specified a target rate of inflation?

For some time now, a number of countries and central banks have announced a target rate of inflation, often in a relatively narrow range. But the Fed had not done so until recently, influenced in part, I would suppose, by the fact that inflation was only one element of its dual legal mandate. An announcement might have raised difficult political and public relations questions about trade-offs between price stability and maximum employment. The institution instead always reaffirmed its commitment to both in general terms, even while shifting its focus from one to the other as required by economic circumstances.

Nonetheless, the institution in recent years has become much more forthcoming and explicit about how it expects various key economic variables to behave in future. That tendency finally reached the point where the Fed, apparently urged along by Chairman Bernanke, has found a way publicly to specify a price target in a low-key way within a context of expectations for other important measures.

For several years, the FOMC had already been publishing, on a quarterly basis, a summary of economic projections (SEP) of key real economic and price variables by each of its members (both voting and nonvoting), although the names are not specified, for two to three years ahead. In addition, even projections for a "longer-run" were included. The key variables encompassed the change in real gross domestic product

(GDP), the most comprehensive measure of the nation's economic growth; the unemployment rate; and two measures of inflation.

This was carried a step further in a Fed announcement (press release dated July 25, 2012) of the FOMC's agreement on "principles regarding its longer-run goals and monetary policy strategy." Principally, prices became not just one among other key variables that were projected but instead were viewed like a specific target. In the Committee's words, the "inflation rate over the longer run is primarily determined by monetary policy, and hence the Committee has the ability to specify a longer-run goal for inflation." The other variables were, it was indicated, much less directly under the control of monetary policy.

The Fed added to the mix what it termed "policy path charts." These showed individual member's (unnamed) judgments about the appropriate timing of the next change in the Committee's target federal funds rate and also their projections about the level of the nominal funds rate at the ends of each of the specified years ahead and in the longer-run as well.

With regard to a goal for inflation, the FOMC went on to note in the press release "that inflation at the rate of 2 percent, as measured by the annual change in the price index for personal consumption expenditures, is most consistent over the longer run with the Federal Reserve's statutory mandate." That index (termed PCE inflation) is derived from and is consistent with the government's calculation of the nation's GDP. It is similar to, but differs in some technical and conceptual ways, from the better known consumer price index (CPI), also published by the government and employed, among other uses, in calculations of inflation adjustments for Social Security payments. Nonetheless, the degree of inflation shown by these two indexes is generally similar.

In short, beginning in 2012, the Fed announced a PCE inflation rate of 2% as its target rate (which was about what the market had in any event long suspected). No range of ups and downs around that rate was given; presumably that will depend on judgments that can only be made in light of actual changing circumstances in the economy.

Some indication of what will enter into the Fed's flexibility in price judgments can be garnered from the other price index for which FOMC makes projections. That is called the core PCE. It represents the PCE excluding food and energy prices. The Fed makes annual projections of that measure but does not provide any longer-run projection since it does not represent the Fed's fundamental goal for price stability.

In the shorter-run, however, the Fed has placed a lot of emphasis on the core. It believes food and energy prices are subject to considerable volatility and may provide misleading indications of underlying inflation. That is certainly true, but the essential question is: misleading for how long?

One answer would be until they are reflected in rising labor costs as consumers seek higher wages to compensate for greater food and travel expenses that undermine their standard of living. After all, people do have to eat and move about. By that time, the more fundamental PCE and its rate of growth may unfortunately have begun to experience a more lasting upward shift as a result of the basic cost-push pressures. Since monetary policy generally works with a long lag, the Fed may then find itself, if it has not moved toward monetary restraint soon enough, more behind the curve than is good for a smooth and effective transition to a more active anti-inflation policy.

Such judgments will, of course, have to be made no matter what particular aggregate price measures are looked at. But a number of countries do not seem to pay as much attention to a core inflation measure as does the Fed in the shorter run, and some make different judgments about what the core should reflect.

4

INSTRUMENTS OF
MONETARY POLICY

*How are the Fed's monetary instruments employed in the
policy process?*

In implementing its monetary policy, the Fed has several policy instruments available to it, principally the open market, discount window, and reserve requirement functions noted earlier. They all work through their influence on availability of reserves that the nation's banks system come to hold behind their deposit liabilities at regional Fed banks. The total amount of these reserves—some required by law, some held to facilitate banks' clearing and payments, some serving as an operating or cautionary buffer—is in the aggregate controllable by the Fed in its role as the country's designated central bank.

The amount of reserves supplied by the Fed in the process of policy implementation and the amount of currency in circulation—both liabilities of the central bank—represent the nation's monetary base. The base is supported for the most part by the Fed's own holdings of U.S. government securities or government-guaranteed securities. From time to time, loans made through the discount window can also be a quite important asset supporting the monetary base and were especially so during the worst of the credit crisis. The ups and downs of the base reflect the extent to which the Fed's monetary policies are working to help expand or restrain, through impacts on the banking system, the nation's credit and money in an effort to achieve its dual economic objectives.

The monetary base comprises over 90% of the Fed's balance sheet, which is put together for the system as a whole and published weekly as the consolidated statement of condition of all 12 regional Reserve Banks. The currency component of the base is automatically provided by the Fed in response to the public's demand for it. As a result, the Fed's monetary policy decisions are reflected in actions that directly affect only the aggregate of bank reserve balances contained in the base.

Reserve balances ran at an exceptionally high 35% to 50% or so of the Fed's balance sheet in the credit crisis period because banks held huge amounts of excess reserves. However, in normal times, banks usually hold far fewer excess reserves, so that the aggregate of bank reserve balances would take up a much smaller share of what would be a considerably reduced balance sheet for the Fed. (See Appendices A-1 and A-2 for examples of the Fed's balance sheet before, during, and after the credit crisis.)[1]

When normalcy does return to banking markets, however, past experience with excess reserves will not be as good a predictor of future behavior as it once was. Since 2008, the Fed has had the authority to pay interest to banks on their excess reserves as well as on their required reserves. Exactly how it will continue to exercise that authority remains to be seen. In announcing its approach, the Fed publicly indicated that it views the interest rate paid on excess reserves as serving monetary policy purposes, while that on required reserves as compensating banks for the implicit tax incurred in holding them.

No matter what the share of bank reserve balances turns out to be on the Fed's balance sheet, it is the Fed's ultimate control over them that is crucial to its enormous power. An individual commercial bank can become more or less aggressive in seeking to enlarge its share of reserves and its share of the banking market, but it is always competing for an amount that can be limited by the Fed.

How much those reserves will expand or contract depends on the operating guide employed by the FOMC in making its policy decisions. The Fed may use one or another type of thermostat, so to speak, to help it decide how much heat to let out of the furnace. For a long time now, that thermostat has been represented by the federal funds rate, although other indicators of money market pressure have been used in the past. However, for the particular purpose of focusing on inflation control under the difficult circumstances of the early 1980s, the Volcker Fed for a while took a radically different approach by taking a predetermined aggregate amount of reserves as an operating guide instead of using a money market guide to set the thermostat.

Which of the Fed's instruments are most significant for implementing policy?

Of the classical policy instruments available to the Fed, open market operations controlled by the FOMC are certainly the most important. As the financial world modernized and became more complex, and banks increasingly shared the stage with other institutions and securities markets, the Fed's market operations moved more and more toward the leading edge of policy implementation—the discount window and reserve requirements normally being employed in supporting roles.

Open market operations have the great advantage of providing the Fed with many easily and continuously implemented operational options. Because of the breadth, depth, and resiliency of the government securities market (to which open market operations are mainly confined by law), they can be undertaken at the FOMC's initiative whenever and in whatever size or form it wishes. In that process, they can also be blended in flexibly as required to offset and neutralize other factors influencing the nation's reserve base. These factors include variations in borrowing at the discount window, currency flows into and out of circulation, and foreign exchange market operations—along with other highly volatile technical factors, like day-to-day ups and downs in U.S. Treasury deposits held at the Fed and in so-called float (timing differences between credits and debits of reserve balance flows among individual banks in the payments process).

Compared with open market operations, the discount window provides less flexibility for monetary policy because reserves provided through that route depend not on the Fed's initiative but on the erratic willingness of member banks to borrow (they generally prefer to obtain needed liquidity in the impersonal federal funds market or other sectors of the money market). Also, from a purely administrative perspective, the discount window entails a rather more complex and cumbersome process than found in the direct and immediate connection between an FOMC policy decision and its implementation by the manager of the system's open market account stationed at the New York Fed.

Finally, as explained in chapter 2, the fundamental regulatory change the Fed Board made to discount window procedures in 2002 provided that the discount rate recommended by Reserve Bank boards has to be set at a premium to the FOMC's targeted funds rate. Whatever the rate charged, however, when financial stabilization issues impede on or overlap with monetary policy operations, the discount window comes into its own and in some circumstances can become the senior partner, as it was during the worst of the recent credit crisis.

Reserve requirement changes, which can be made at the initiative of the Fed's Board of Governors, are simply not suitable for use on a continuing basis in today's fast-moving financial world in which banks face broad competition for their services. A single change in requirements may be appropriate from time to time, but continual modifications would tend to disrupt planning of a bank's business model, creating unnecessary uncertainties and hesitancies.

Reserve requirements in the United States these days can best be thought of as a useful fulcrum that helps the account manager in New York attain his federal funds target with more ease and precision. Because reserve requirements are based on earlier deposits (the bulk are lagged by two weeks), the Fed at least knows with reasonable certainty the amount of reserves needed in the banking system to meet those requirements during a so-called two-week reserve maintenance period. That fulcrum can be used as a starting point in gauging the volume and direction (whether adding to or subtracting from reserve balances) of open market operations that will yield the target federal funds rate.

Since the credit crisis erupted, the Fed has acquired certain other policy instruments. It can now offer term deposits (about one month in maturity so far) in which banks can place funds with Federal Reserve Banks. When banks place funds in these deposits, their reserve balances are immediately reduced; the nation's monetary base declines while not altering the Fed's aggregate liabilities to banks and the size of its balance sheet. Also, as noted above, the Fed is now permitted to pay a market-related interest rate to banks on their excess and required reserve holdings (about 0.25% on both in the credit crisis period).

Neither the ability to offer term deposits nor the interest rate on excess reserves would appear to alter the primacy of traditional policy instruments. Nonetheless, both may well be of considerable value when economic normalcy becomes more apparent and the time comes for the Fed to cut back on the monetary base while also beginning to raise the funds rate from its near-zero floor.

How are open market operations employed in policy implementation?

The Fed's policy strategy is set through a policy directive issued by the FOMC normally about eight times per year that directs the Federal Reserve Bank of New York to carry out the decisions made at its most recent meeting.

For the most part, in recent decades, as already stressed, instructions for open market operations focused almost solely on attainment of reserve conditions consistent with a specific funds rate objective. Such a strategy has, of course, been virtually dormant in the United States since the height of the credit crisis in late 2008 and early 2009, with the federal funds rate subsequently remaining at a rock bottom zero to one-quarter of a percent range through 2012. It will probably revive when economic recovery shows clear staying power. The funds rate had in fact fluctuated widely during the past five decades, reaching an unusually high peak in the area of 15–20% in the vigorous inflation-fighting years of the early 1980s, while fluctuating mostly in the vicinity of a 2–7% range in other postwar years.

Using the funds rate and associated money market conditions as an operating objective permits the Fed to fulfill its basic central banking function of maintaining adequate liquidity to sustain the economy and day-to-day market functioning while also influencing the overall supply of credit as needed to achieve its economic objectives over time. Setting aside major credit crisis periods when exceptional actions are required, it also has the advantage of minimizing interference in market processes that efficiently balance credit supplies and demands among uses that best satisfy the tastes and needs of businesses, consumers, investors, and savers in the constantly evolving dynamics of our enterprise economy. Presumably for similar reasons, most major central banks in advanced economies appear to focus on money market conditions, expressed one way or another, as their day-to-day objective.

The Fed's policy directive also includes whatever other instructions may be needed to guide the intermeeting actions of the account manager. Most recently for instance, in the aftermath of the credit crisis, they encompassed directions about buying and selling securities for other particular purposes, such as acquiring longer-term government and mortgage-related issues to help economic recovery along.

The account manager's market security transactions can readily be employed to reach the FOMC's fund rate objective since they are paid for through debits or credits to bank reserve balances held at the Fed. The funds rate then goes up, down, or stays the same to reflect the net effect of how the Fed's buying and selling transactions change the total availability of reserves available to the banking system relative to the demand for them from the banks. Moreover, because of the size and absorptive capacity of the government market, the Fed has little trouble in seamlessly accomplishing what it needs to do, without significant lasting impacts on the government securities market (except to the extent that the market comes to believe a change in policy may be in process or in the offing).

How does the federal funds rate connect with money market conditions in general?

The fed funds rate is one of a collection of rates that comprise the money market, a market made up of diverse borrowers and lenders with banks essentially serving as its backstop. These include large businesses that issue their own commercial paper and also place surplus funds in other money market instruments; the U.S. government that funds its financing need in part through Treasury bills that are short-term (up to one year in maturity) and attractive to various institutions and others for liquidity purposes; security and commodity dealers who require short-term loans to fund inventories as part of their market-making activity; and myriad borrowers and lenders for any number of purposes, some more speculative than others.

Because of the central bank's well-understood power to step in and do what is needed to set any rate it wishes (within a narrow range of fluctuation), the funds rate unequivocally functions as the key rate in the money market. With the discount rate set at a penalty to it, the funds rate is the lowest rate banks can pay to obtain funds urgently and unexpectedly needed by their customers to meet business or other obligations. It is the rate that closely influences the pricing of other money market rates—such as, to name a few, rates for commercial paper, dealer loans, and U.S. Treasury bills. (Since federal funds transactions are not traditionally collateralized, they do not always trade at the lowest rate in their maturity sector of the market.)

The ability of the banking system to stand as a reliable focal point for the money market depends to a great extent on an efficient, well-functioning interbank market. Such a market permits the reserve balances held at Fed banks by member banks and other depository institutions to be moved daily in large volume around the country in response to shifting needs. On balance, smaller banks traditionally have reserve surpluses that can be loaned out, while larger nationwide banks, which tend to run sophisticated and aggressive operations, are more likely to need funds on any given day. They are subject to the volatile day-to-day demands on their facilities from larger and very active customers, especially so in New York and major regional financial centers.

While the Fed's operating target for open market operations has been expressed as a federal funds rate in recent decades, in earlier times—particularly when the discount window at the Fed was structured very differently from now—some numerical measure of liquidity pressures on banks, like member banks' borrowing at the Fed or so-called net free reserves (the difference between excess reserves and member bank borrowing), was employed as a guide rather than a specific rate. Such liquidity measures were for much of the time reasonably well correlated with money market rate behavior generally.

However, a money market rate, like that on federal funds, is a significantly better overall guide for open market operations than a particular quantitative measure of bank liquidity. Use of such a measure would be counterproductive, for example, if banks' attitudes toward their own liquidity needs changed from their norm. For instance, if banks' lost confidence in their financial positions for whatever reason and wished to hold more liquidity, the Fed would find money market conditions tightening unless it quickly made its own liquidity target more generous. If a funds rate instead had been taken as a target, open market operations would automatically provide the additional reserves (instead of involving the delays and complexities of another policy meeting and decision). Market developments would force the account manager to supply the additional reserves needed to accommodate banks' greater liquidity demands and keep the rate from rising.

How does the funds rate decision affect other credit markets?

The effect on money market rates of an FOMC decision is, of course, only the beginning of a story that works its way among many markets and which in the end influences spending and saving decisions basic to the economy, although with variable lags and uncertain intensity. Money market rates are the base rates in the economy, but not the rates that have the most direct effect on whether spending will become stronger or weaker over time. The impact of interest rates on spending occurs to a greater extent in other markets, especially longer-term credit markets where housing and business capital outlays for plant and equipment are financed, as well as in the shorter-term consumer finance markets.

Money market rates are often, but not always, the lowest ones in the nation's market and financial system. When lowest, the structure of yields by maturity (from short to long) and by credit quality (by perceived degree of credit risk from low to high) that encompasses and cuts across the major credit and security markets in the country rises from there. The yield curve is said to be upward sloping.

However, as the Fed tightens policy and short-term rates rise commensurately, at some point markets will believe that they have peaked or soon will, and longer-term rates will begin rising less than they had or begin declining. They will antici- pate lower short-term rates in the future as policy's efforts to moderate the economy begin succeeding, credit demands abate, and the economy weakens. The yield curve will flatten out and then become downward sloping for a while until con- ditions for a more natural upward slope take over.

The Fed often stresses the need to keep inflation expecta- tions, an important influence on the yield curve, in check as a major influence on their policies. When volatile, they com- pound problems of maintaining a satisfactory balance in meet- ing monetary policy's dual economic mandate.

For instance, if the market comes to expect more inflation in the future even while the economy is still producing well below its capacity, longer-term yields will tend to rise in anticipation and potentially work against a further economic recovery that may be in process. Also, the more deeply inflation expectations become embedded in interactive wage and price decision- making as the economy approaches full capacity, the harder it will be for policy to curb inflation without serious recessionary repercussions, such as occurred in the early 1980s.

How do key borrowers respond to changed market conditions?

In general, the Fed's influence on spending in the country and its ability to attain its dual economic mandate without too much social and economic disruption depends not only on the timeliness with which the FOMC alters money market condi- tions and the response of broader markets to such changes. It also, and importantly, depends on how sensitively borrowers in such markets respond to changes of interest rates and other related financial incentives.

To the extent borrowers and their associated spending are less responsive to interest rate changes, the less effective will monetary policy be, for instance, in encouraging an economic recovery. More direct methods of stimulating the economy, such as the tax and expenditure powers of governmental fiscal policy, will be needed.

Long-lived capital outlays tend to be the most interest sensitive areas of the private economy and are affected mainly by longer-term interest rates. Housing outlays, for example, are affected by mortgage market rates as well as a host of other factors (e.g., down-payment requirements). During the postwar period, renewed housing expansion often spurred the economy out of recession, but by the same token, periodic drops in housing outlays also led the economy into recession— most recently, of course, an all too memorable one. Business spending on plant and equipment also has been responsive to the longer-term cost of capital as indicated by corporate bond yields and the cost of issuing equity, though perhaps not quite as much as housing. Businesses, at least large ones, often have access to large internal fund flows (saving in effect) not typical of prospective homeowners.

Setting investment in housing apart, consumer spending, much of which is for current not future needs, seems relatively less sensitive to interest rates. Spending on durables, like autos, is clearly dependent to an important degree on the availability and cost of shorter-term credit. But the bulk of consumer outlays is for ordinary living purposes and financed out of current income flows.

As a whole, current spending by consumers is less likely than housing and business capital outlays to galvanize an economic recovery or a recession. It can to a degree, of course, as optimism rises or wanes, but it is mostly a passive force dependent on incoming family earnings.

Spending by the federal government is little, if at all, dependent on interest costs and more dependent on the political philosophies and politics influencing budgetary decisions. Indeed, as already noted, the government's fiscal policy is the nation's other major macro-economic tool and serves a complementary role with the Fed for maintaining economic stability and growth. In that respect, it played a mixed and spotty role, both here and in Europe, during the recent credit crises and aftermath.

State and local government spending too is heavily influenced by politics but also by revenue streams that rise and fall along with the national economy. For the latter reason, such spending often is pro-cyclical. However, outlays probably tend to be encouraged a little by lower interest rates that permit debt service to take up less room in restricted budgets.

While some sectors of the economy are inherently more sensitive than others to interest rate changes, all may become more or less so relative to their norm at particular times for a number of reasons. It can depend on market expectations of how much more money market tightening (or easing) is in store. It can depend on expectations about the strength (or weakness) of the overall economy and employment in the periods ahead. It can depend on confidence that inflation is restrained. It can depend on expectations about how federal government budget policies are likely to evolve. It can depend on perceived developments in the rest of the world. It can depend, most particularly, on broad political, cultural, and social factors that can make or break confidence in the future and make people and institutions more or less conservative or liberal in their decisions about spending and saving.

How do FOMC policy decisions adapt to market uncertainties?

The only real option it has is watchful waiting. Central banking is inherently a conservative trade.

The Fed can keep careful track of how markets are responding relative to expectations through access to its own economic models, to those from many other sources, and to a large staff which is alert to a continuous flow of current information for assessing how current developments seem to be evolving—whether faster or slower than normal, whether radically different, or, as I have heard from children and grandchildren, whatever.

Given all of the lags and uncertainties involved, the effects of monetary policy as it is being implemented cannot be easily foretold. It is simply the case that monetary policy will ever be subject to adjustments made on the go as it becomes clearer and clearer how the credit markets and the economy are in fact responding to the circumstances of the time.

How do open market operations avoid creating too much money and inflation?

It is far from easy to measure with any certainty the empirical counterpart of the "money" referred to in the saying noted early on that inflation is caused by too much money chasing too few goods. A very traditional view of the nation's stock of money in the hands of the public would be represented by the amount of currency in circulation plus the amount of checkable demand deposits held at banks and other depository institutions. They both serve the traditional functions of money as a means of payment and store of value (and also a unit of account). They can both be instantly employed to purchase good and services and also settle financial transactions; they also represent a store of value that is considered safe insofar as their face value is not at risk (although obviously their real values are influenced by changes up or down in the average level of prices).

Over the years, however, as the nation's banking system and overall financial structure evolved, especially in the 1970s and after, other financial instruments developed that could in some degree serve akin to a traditional money purpose. Those that seemed close enough in function were, in monetary policy talk, considered "near-monies." When deemed particularly close to traditional money, they were added to currency and demand deposits, yielding a second measure of money—and those less close making a third such measure, not to mention additional others investigated that seemed conceptually possible until the outer limits of common sense were finally reached.

In light of experience gained as time went on with public attitudes and behavior toward the more diverse and sophisticated array of money substitutes and financial outlets, the Fed now publishes only two money measures, one narrow and one somewhat broader—M1 and M2. The former comprises currency in circulation in the hands of the public, demand deposits at commercial banks, and other checking deposits at various depository institutions. M2 is broadened to include closely related types of accounts that can be quickly accessed by the public and transferred into deposits used in settling transactions. They include other deposit-like instruments, such as savings accounts, small-denomination time deposits, and balances held at retail money market funds.

While the near-monies included in M2 are like traditional money—their face value is not usually deemed at risk and they can be quickly withdrawn for making payments—they, more so than the components of M1, also include funds set aside for longer-term purposes, like saving for a home down payment or general retirement needs. Consequently, M2 is more than four times as large as M1—and possible candidates for broader M's are larger yet.

Of the two measures, M1 in an arithmetic sense is most closely connected to the Fed's monetary base, since its deposit components are subject to reserve requirements. In an economic sense, though, the value of money measures for judging or formulating monetary policy has little to do with how closely they are directly connected to the monetary base. Rather, it depends on how useful they are for predicting with any reasonable degree of certainty the likely course of inflation or in assessing the adequacy of Fed efforts to avert or moderate shorter-run or cyclical economic instabilities.

Over the years, there has been much and often-heated debate and related research among economists outside and within central banks about the importance of money supply as a guide to policy as compared with interest rates (often characterized as monetarists vs. Keynesians), not to mention which particular measure(s) of money would best serve that purpose (monetarists vs. monetarists in that case). It is difficult, in a short space, to generalize about the issues and do justice to the various views held, but it seems fair to say that the debate has by now greatly calmed down.

In part, I believe this is owed to the difficulties over the years in empirically finding a measure of money (whether narrow, broad, or broader) that consistently anticipates the timing and strength of future inflation. It is also hard to find one that consistently shows a stable, predictable relationship to the nominal value of goods and services produced in the economy or to the level of interest rates.

The public's demand for money (economic speak for "wish to hold money") in relation to the size of the economy no longer seems consistent enough (if it ever was) to provide monetary policy with a clear guide for its operations. Rather, money demand seems more to evolve uncertainly through market processes as the public adjusts its liquidity, borrowing, and longer-run saving and investment propensities to the emerging circumstances of the time—including newly developing market technology and all the political and other developments that can influence expectations about the future and confidence in the economy.

Moreover, banks have become less dominant in financial markets as unique repositories of the nation's money through offerings of demand and savings deposits. Spurred on by competition and emerging financial opportunities, banks spread their wings broadly into more sophisticated areas of finance, partly through participation in financial holding companies open to securities and other related businesses where the public had increasingly entrusted its savings.

It now appears that something like "money" can be found throughout virtually all sectors of financial markets—certainly in some of the near-monies just beyond those included in the Fed's M2, like large certificates of deposit mainly held by businesses and wealthy individuals and even further beyond in various risk assets in securities markets. At least until the credit crisis gave out a warning signal, the public apparently also had come to view riskier longer-term assets, such as holdings in stock funds and the amount of home equity, as serving something like the same functions as old-fashioned money or near-monies. At a minimum, some unknown, probably small, portion of them were viewed as readily available for spending—the ease of getting cash by borrowing against home equity being one example.

As a general point, there is indeed, at least conceptually, a kind of money out there chasing too few goods if inflation is becoming a problem, or too little money if the economy is weak. But that money seems well disguised and cannot be reliably found and counted, if it ever really could.

It can be seen however, after the fact, in the degree to which the traditional measures turn over, that is, in the volume of checks written against bank deposits. For instance, a check written against one's account in a mutual fund is ultimately cleared through a bank. The more such accounts are used the higher the turnover in the checkable deposits at banks through which payments are ultimately made and the less used the smaller the turnover. In other words, inflation can be financed from a higher turnover of the Fed's measure of M1 and also of M2, in reflection of the money-like components embodied in the huge volume of financial assets held by the public outside those relatively narrow measures.

In one way or another, through one route or another, more money is chasing too few goods but not in any very predictable or stable pattern.

All the instabilities and uncertainties about the public's attitudes toward "money" and its use are yet another reason that the Fed, and practically all other major central banks, normally implements monetary policy through gradual changes in interest rates and credit market conditions as economic conditions warrant. The amount of "money" which emerges in the economy from that process, not measurable with any precision, will depend on the interest and income sensitivity of the demand for money that happens to evolve under the varying circumstances of the time. The interest sensitivity, such as it turns out to be, will respond to spreads between yields on deposits to competing forms of assets, some near-monies and some not so near at all. The income sensitivity to a great extent will be influenced over time by ongoing technological and other changes (credit cards, debit cards, and the like) that permit cash holdings to be economized.

With all the uncertainties about the behavior of money in the hands of the public it is no wonder that the Fed's current approach to evaluating inflation risks seems to be the eminently practical one of observing how close the real output of the economy is coming to its potential output. The closer the more likely inflation will become a problem.

Still, it might be well to look over one's shoulder at some measure of money supply in the hands of the public as a checkpoint in the process. I would suppose some FOMC members might and some might not. No matter, there are other market guides, like measures of inflation expectations implicit in the pricing of inflation-indexed bonds, that provide supplemental, perhaps even better, indicators of inflation to come. Measurable money's track record has been less than stellar in recent decades.

Does the money market itself influence spending or is it mostly a policy conduit?

While the bigger picture described above appears to play down the role of the money market by making it seem mainly a conduit for the successive steps through which policy unfolds, there is more to its role than that. Fundamentally, it performs an important stabilizing function for the economy. It is something like the oil that keeps economic wheels moving along, sometimes slower sometimes faster, but at least moving. Indeed, emerging countries seeking to accelerate economic development are advised to work toward a competitive domestic interbank market as a very early step toward establishing a pro-growth and stabilizing financial infrastructure.

In that broad context, should signs of faltering appear within the money market itself, they can be a serious indication of deeper troubles beneath the surface not yet clearly evident in other markets—something like an early warning signal. In 2007, for example, trading in longer-term maturities in the interbank federal funds market began drying up—in retrospect, clearly a sign that a serious confidence crisis could be showing its potential in the traditionally most liquid of banking and money markets.

It would seem that lending banks were beginning to have some doubts about credit risks in the portfolios of borrowing banks and were backing away from lending their reserve balances except at very, very short-term. To avoid the potential for any serious disruptions in the banking system's important function of ensuring the day-to-day liquidity required by the economy, the Fed, late in the year, finally implemented a system by which banks could in effect bid at the discount window for the longer-term federal funds that were becoming harder to borrow in the market.

As the credit crisis came upon us in full force in late 2008 and early 2009, when the funds rate was already at around zero, other elements of the money market gave clear signals of a widespread breakdown in confidence. For instance, some money market funds were unable to maintain par values in face of growing withdrawals by the public (they "broke the buck" in the expression of the day), and sharp upward dollar interest rate thrusts occurred in the widely watched London market for short-term interbank borrowing (LIBOR).[2] These signs of lost confidence in usually extremely safe investments by active market participants thought to "be in the know" were disturbing tremors of greater underlying quakes potentially in process.

In the end, the huge loss of confidence in financial institutions, the government, the Congress, and the Fed that ultimately infected the public and deepened the crisis had more fundamental causes. Regulatory laxness in the housing market (among others) and widespread tolerance of excess leverage by key financial executives in highly interconnected markets are among them. But high on this writer's list would be the apparent inability of those at the helm of governmental and large private institutions to sense the magnitude of the crisis that might come and, once it came, the evident hesitancy and lack of preparedness shown in dealing with it. The loss of confidence made the recession much more severe than it need have been and contributed to the long-lasting sluggishness of the recovery.

Monetary policy was handicapped in its ability to stimulate recovery, because the public became much less willing than usual to borrow and spend as interest rates came down and stayed down, and as banks and other institutions for a long period remained less-willing lenders than usual even as liquidity became abundant. The Fed for a time was forced to devote an enormous amount of its lending resources to shoring up the short-term market and keeping the money markets patched together. Maintaining a reasonably well-functioning money market was a sine qua non if the Fed's normal instruments of monetary policy were to help in turning the economy toward recovery.

Are the Fed's powers also used to influence the government securities market?

Looking back as far as the Second World War, there have been three noteworthy periods when the process of open market operations has diverged from the norm of simply aiming at money market conditions, whether indexed by the federal funds rate or some other proxy for those conditions, or aimed at some other specific bank reserve objective.

In the first instance, during and shortly after the Second World War, the Fed helped the government finance its huge wartime expenditures by agreeing to purchase longer-term Treasury bonds as needed to keep their interest rate from rising above a specified low level (2.5% at the time) and also to maintain a much lower Treasury bill rate. This agreement was tantamount to monetizing the government debt and the Fed effectively lost its monetary policy independence. Any time yields rose above those rates, the Fed would have to create money to buy the securities. Open market operations were at the will of the public rather than the will of the Fed. In such circumstances, the Fed would not be able to control inflation by limiting expansion of the nation's monetary base.

The famous accord reached with the Treasury in early 1951 restored the Fed's full freedom to determine monetary policy independently. By eliminating the agreement on Treasury bond rates (the peg on Treasury bills had been eliminated a few years earlier), the FOMC regained full powers to manage open market operations as it saw fit to keep inflation under control.

In the early 1960s, the Fed agreed to another, and much less dramatic, effort to manage its government securities portfolio for special purposes. The Fed then agreed with the Treasury to engage in a so-called operation twist of the government securities market. The idea was twofold: (1) push down longer-term rates to help keep the domestic economy expanding; and (2) avoid a drop in short-term rates to avert a weakening dollar on exchange markets; the fear was that a weaker dollar would exert upward pressure on inflation and diminish confidence in economy.

The Fed purchased longer-term Treasury debt but sold an equivalent amount shorter-term Treasury notes, so that there was no net effect from that restructuring of its portfolio on the monetary base. The Treasury, for its part, concentrated more of its new financing in the short-term area relative to longer-term issues, among other things flexibly raising three-month T-bill offerings to shore up that rate.

Day-to-day open market operations continued to focus on relatively tight money market conditions, and day-to-day open market operations were conducted to keep bank liquidity positions at least as tight as before. For a while, the three-month Treasury bill rate was taken as the flagship rate in assessing overall money market conditions.

Whether operation twist was successful has been subject to considerable debate over the years. It does seem to have lowered longer-term rates on government securities and related private rates (for which risk-free government bonds traditionally provide something of a benchmark) for a short while. Corporate bonds issuance picked up for a time as the retirement of longer-term government debt initially made it easier for private borrowers to raise capital. But soon the twist effect on longer-term rates wore off, and the rates again began to reflect such fundamental influences as expected real economic growth and inflation over time.

Most recently, during the credit crisis and its aftermath, the Fed has made a huge and sustained effort to purchase longer-term government and government-guaranteed mortgage-related debt instruments in an effort to reduce their rates. With yields on risk-free government debt the bellwether rate in markets, it was hoped to lower borrowing costs, particularly in the mortgage market but also presumably in the corporate bond market to encourage recovery once the credit crisis came under control in the spring of 2009. By the end of 2012, more than $2 trillion of long-term Treasury notes and bonds, issues of federal housing agencies, and mortgage-backed securities guaranteed by the government had been added on balance to the Fed's portfolio. They became the principal source of the massive expansion in the Fed's balance sheet that had been crucial to containing the crisis and helping the sluggish recovery along.

In order to limit the rise in the nation's monetary base, however, several hundred billion dollars of gross purchases had been offset by sales of shorter-term Treasury notes. This relatively limited aspect of the policy was similar to the Fed's role in operation twist of the early 1960s.

While the policy appeared to have reduced longer-term rates to an extent, it is not clear how much was caused by the Fed's monetization of Treasury debt or how much by continued weak conditions in the mortgage market, the sluggish recovery of the economy, and private credit demands more generally. In any event, because the Fed's target funds rate, and associated money market conditions, remained at the market minimum of around 0% during that whole period, any further monetary ease to support economic recovery perforce had to take the form of a sharp, historically unique expansion in the Fed's balance sheet and debt monetization—a policy dubbed quantitative expansion (q.e.) at the time. Most recently, the Fed announced the prospect of further substantial additions to its long-term securities portfolio in 2013.

Nonetheless, at some point when the economy strengthens further, expansionary monetary policy will obviously have to be reversed and some of this excess liquidity removed from markets if the target fed funds rate is to rise. The Fed has the tools to do so, but how and when they will be exercised, and whether they are timely enough remains unknown as of this writing.

Notes

1   Appendices A-1 and A-2 show four examples of the Fed's balance sheet, its key components for policy analysis, and their relation to reserve balances. The examples are for specific dates chosen to illustrate (in A-1) normal conditions in the balance sheet before the credit crisis and then conditions just prior to the distinct worsening of the crisis after mid-September 2008, and (in A-2) the exceptionally massive expansion in the balance sheet as the crisis peaked around mid-December and that even rose further, though transformed in its source, in the Fed's accounts after nearly four years of sluggish economic recovery.

2   The LIBOR market is currently under suspicion of misreporting prices. But there is little doubt that the cost of dollar borrowing in the market rose sharply at the time, whether or not truly reflected by the actual figures banking institutions' reported in the circumstances.

5

THE FORMULATION AND
COMMUNICATION OF
MONETARY POLICY

What is the institutional structure for monetary policy decisions?

Monetary policy is essentially formulated in the FOMC because it is the entity within the Fed that controls open market operations. But of course, as noted earlier, the economic objectives of monetary policy stipulated in the Federal Reserve Act are given to both the FOMC and the Board of Governors of the Fed. Moreover, the Board has control over the other instruments of monetary policy.

In addition, the Board—because of its ultimate control over lending at discount windows and also regulatory and supervisory policies—is the key player in the Fed's implicit policy goal of seeking to ensure systemic stability in banking and financial markets. But all these operations also involve cooperation and understanding of Reserve Bank boards and, of course, regional supervisory staffs. Thus, it is no exaggeration to say that monetary policy in practice involves timely system-wide interactions and actions under the leadership of the Board and its chairman.

There are numerous system-wide meetings on various subjects, such as discount window operations, clearing and payments system issues, and supervisory practices, at various levels of responsibility on regular and ad hoc bases. However, the crucial regular meetings on monetary policy are held by the FOMC normally eight times per year in the large boardroom on the second floor of the original Board building. It is an impressive room with an imposing elliptical mahogany table—long, dark, with an oblong granite center—that expresses solidity, seriousness, and authority. The chairman sits at the head of the table, having entered to begin the meeting from the rear door of his office that adjoins the boardroom.

A large number of attendees fit around the table. They include the Committee's 12 voting members and the seven nonvoting presidents. They also regularly comprise key staff with responsibilities for record keeping, for needed background information on policy discussions, and for implementing the decisions made. This includes the secretary of the Committee and a deputy, the manager of the system's open market account, the principal economists of the Committee, and its legal counsel. They are available to brief the Committee in areas of their expertise and to respond to questions that may arise in the course of Committee discussions.

A substantial number of other staff with important roles in preparing policy analyses sit along the sides of the room, among them several other economists from the Board, an economic aide to each of the Reserve Bank presidents, and others who may be needed for special topics at particular times (and who may attend only parts of a meeting). A number of credit and banking experts from the staff were also in attendance during the height of the credit crisis period. Their inputs helped the FOMC thoroughly understand the background for major lending decisions undertaken by the Board and their impact on the Fed's balance sheet and the nation's monetary base, key measures in gauging monetary policy.

While the FOMC has no legal control over emergency lending programs put into effect to alleviate the credit crisis, it does have the authority to limit their aggregate credit- and liquidity-creating effects if it wishes. Of course, the FOMC would have had little practical reason to limit the credit-enhancing effect of emergency lending operations in a credit-starved economy. But it was important for the Committee to have a firsthand understanding of how much credit was being created, its likely impact on financial markets and the economy, and potential implications for the policy mechanism as the situation changed (presumably for the better).

On occasion, over the course of the crisis and its aftermath, joint meetings of the Board and the FOMC were even held, in which case members of the Board secretariat were present along with members of the FOMC secretariat. One might envision simpler ways of running this particular railroad. But the diverse centers of powers within the Fed work well together because of the cooperative culture within the system and, of course, the practical centrality to its work of the Board of Governors and its chairman.

What material is provided to the FOMC for discussion of the economic outlook?

As background to its discussion of the economy and its outlook, the members of the FOMC will have digested the basic forecasts of economic growth and price behavior looking ahead two to three years contained in the green book—a document of up to 200 pages, all told, prepared by the Board's staff. It reviews and tabulates (in text, charts, and tables) current trends, modified as needed by very most recent developments, in virtually every sector of business and finance of our huge and complex economy. It draws them together to work out a basic staff forecast for the economy, with the help of econometric models of how the economy has performed in the past along with large and necessary dollops of educated judgment regarding the particular circumstances of the current economic environment.

There are many experts on the staff covering important economic areas such as consumer spending, business capital outlays, housing starts and conditions, state and local government developments, federal government spending and tax collections, and international factors influencing exports and imports. They are up to speed on how spending has been evolving, and prospects for the future in their areas in response to the financial, psychological, and political conditions that are distinguishing characteristics of the current economic circumstances under consideration (as compared with earlier ones). Needless to say, there are also experts assigned to follow trends in finance, including banking and capital markets. They are familiar with the evolving availability and cost of credit to fund businesses and consumers, changing market attitudes toward both lending and borrowing, and tendencies in equity markets than can mirror or influence confidence in the nation's economic future as well as the actual current cost of raising capital.

All this information is put on the table, intensively analyzed, and goes into the green book analyses and staff projections of the future. Thus, the forecasts represent the staff's best judgment from interweaving a model-based understanding of economic and financial relationships on average over time with the ongoing knowledge of current developments that reflect the particular circumstances of the world today that policy is dealing with. In the end, the forecast homes in on economic measures crucial to the Committee's dual objectives of maximum employment and price stability—the rate of real economic growth, inflation, and the maximum level of employment (as reflected in the unemployment rate).

There is considerable room for judgments and differences of opinion about the staff's basic economic forecast. It can be shaded one way or another depending on beliefs about certain particular developments in a current economic situation—such as how strong foreign economies will be and their feedback effects on our growth; when can a housing cycle be expected to turn and how strongly; is the potential for growth in domestic output, as influenced by productivity and labor force expansion, being under- or overestimated. Indeed, the green book provides alternative forecasts based on other fundamental assumptions to provide additional background information for the Committee's own discussion of its economic outlook.

Based on a review of green books that have most recently been published as of this writing (those for the year 2006), these alternatives include forecasts based on such reasonable alternative assumptions as a lower so-called NAIRU (the acronym employed by economists for the rate of unemployment below which inflation is very likely to intensify); greater wage acceleration; stronger growth; an extended housing decline; tighter financial conditions (the staff's basic forecast assumes, among other financial conditions, that the FOMC's federal funds rate objective is essentially the most recent one with room for some modest variation looking ahead).

Having such alternatives at hand helps deepen, one would think, the Committee's consideration of the economic outlook. They bear on important issues for policy and help provide a basis for members to understand the economic implications of developments that they might feel are not adequately accounted for in the staff's basic economic forecast.

What material is provided to help the Committee form its monetary policy decision?

Within the context of its outlook for the economy and inflation, the Committee must decide whether to modify its policy course and the strategy with which it has been implemented. That in normal times boils down to a decision about whether actually to change its operating objective for the federal funds rate or to provide other indications of a potential attitudinal shift in policy intentions.

The Committee makes its judgments in that regard aided by the blue book, a 30- to 40-page document from the Board staff made available along with the green book. The nature of the blue book, like its green partner, has evolved over time. Over the past decade or two, while of course retaining and enlarging their very practical focus, they have also taken on some aspects of complex and sophisticated economic texts (one might almost say treatises). This is consistent with the considerable amount of further economic research and advances in understanding that have taken place in the field of monetary economics and policy, yielding a growing body of insights and a greater facility in testing and exploring various alternative approaches and hypotheses. It is also consistent with the growing influence of highly trained economists in key policymaking positions on the Board and at Reserve Banks.

These developments are not without risk, however. The chief one is the possibility that the models and other statistical analyses behind the various findings will subtly work to limit policymakers' horizons, by confining their thinking and tending to divert it from the many cultural and broad market influences on how monetary policy in practice interacts with the economy. One might ask, for instance, why the Fed did not quite sense the huge market dangers, evident in retrospect, behind its policies, regulatory conditions, and within the broad culture of finance in the late 1990s and the opening years of the new century? Models and statistical analyses represent advanced, useful tools for evaluating monetary policy, but the mysterious capacity for contextual judgment remains, in this writer's view, the trump card.

Be that as it may, the blue book, in addition to presenting policy alternatives for the Committee's consideration, also contains relevant analyses of how the alternatives compare to certain policy rules that have been proposed by various economists and seem useful for background consideration. These include a few variations on the so-called Taylor rule, an innovative and influential piece of thinking published about two decades ago by a well-known economist that econometrically determined a funds rate most consistent with the output gap and the Fed's desired goal for inflation (in effect a real funds rate). Also for background and comparative purposes, and hearkening back to older monetarist-type rules, blue books also include model-based projections of the money supply (M2 in this case) econometrically associated with policy alternatives. For good measure, blue books also have included elaborately derived estimates (in a wide range of variation) of equilibrium real federal funds rates consistent with maintaining output at its potential over time while keeping inflation under control.

Valuable as these background factors may be to individual Committee members, the blue book's basic task is to put forward reasonable alternatives that serve as a starting point for policy discussion at the meeting. There are often three that cover raising, lowering, or keeping the nominal funds rate the same. Or if the situation is obvious enough, they might involve no change in the rate and other options that might involve only easing or tightening.

Over the past decade or so, however, the Fed has been intent on providing some indication of how policy might evolve in the future in connection with its operating decision. As a result, the policy alternatives presented to the Committee also have included options for associated explanatory wording about how its funds rate decision is connected with emerging inflation or other economic indicators at the time that could tilt future decisions one way or another. For instance, there could be two policy alternatives for the Committee that would leave the existing funds rate unchanged, but one might be accompanied by revised wording that suggests (with all necessary delicacy) a bit more worry about risks of inflation ahead.

How do Committee members conduct their discussion of the economy and monetary policy?

After the chairman brings the Committee to order, the manager of the system open market account is traditionally called upon to review the implementation of policy operations following the previous meeting and respond to any questions about them. After that, the Committee turns to its main business of what adjustments, if any, need to be made in its policy strategy for the roughly six-week intermeeting period ahead.

Before turning to that crucial issue, Committee members will have heard a summary staff presentation of recent key economic developments and their implication for the staff's economic outlook as detailed in the green book. Following what can be a probing and relatively extended period in which members seek clarification from the staff on any particular questions that may concern them, all 19 participate in a go-round and express, in some detail, their own views about the economy and its outlook. Each participant makes a statement, based on his or her perspective, with Reserve Bank presidents focusing on the national picture, though at times including brief references to regional developments (which have already been released to the public in some detail in what is termed the beige book).

Each participant will give his or her own opinion about whether the economy is moving along on the same track as thought previously and whether inflation is or is not becoming more or less of a problem in light of more recent economic data and other information. The views will differ in one way or another from the staff presentation and from one another. From those statements and further discussions, it is up to the chairman to work out and seek agreement on some sort of consensus that can be taken to represent the viewpoint of the Committee, or at least a majority of its voting members.

(This discussion and other parts of the meeting are included in a nearly verbatim transcript that is released along with the relevant green and blue books with a rather long lag, averaging roughly five and a half years, given that one full year's batch of transcripts is released all at once. Well before that, however, the minutes of each meeting, including an extended summary of economic and policy discussions, are released to the public about two weeks after each meeting. But unlike the transcript, no names are referred to in the very useful summary of discussion contained in the minutes. Variant views are described as "one member," "a few," or "some"; only dissenters have the opportunity for a brief statement of their views in connection with the vote on policy recorded in the minutes.)

After reviewing the economy, the Committee turns to its discussion of policy. There will first be an opportunity for members to raise whatever questions they want with the senior staff person responsible for the blue book and for the summary oral presentation at the meeting. Following that, members turn to a discussion of policy, whether it should be changed, and if so, how. The chairman may offer his views in the course of discussion. Depending on his temperament and the situation, he may wait until the end of the preliminary discussion of policy to summarize how he sees a consensus developing, or he might offer some views of his own either for clarification or possibly influence.

Regardless, it is the job of the chairman at some point toward the end of the meeting to propose for consideration by the voting members an operating directive to the account manager that will contain the Federal funds rate objective for the forthcoming intermeeting period as well as any other instructions that affect the Fed's portfolio, such as those involved with the recent post credit crisis efforts that greatly increased holdings of longer-term securities and the Fed's monetary base. Further discussion might ensue. In the end, that proposed directive, or some variant of it, will be voted up or down, normally up by that point, although there may be some dissents, usually not much more than one or two.

In addition, it is up to the chairman to obtain a vote on the wording of the press release to be issued right after FOMC meeting that conveys the full dimensions of the policy stance adopted going beyond the specific operating instructions.

What, in general, are the main influences on the Fed's policy decision?

Many things influence the Fed's decision on monetary policy at any particular meeting but the most important, I would judge in normal times, are clearly the outlooks for the economy and inflation. Voting members must continuously bear in mind whether their decision is consistent with the dual economic mandate given to them by law.

Of course, in periods of major crises, such as the great inflation and credit crises of the postwar years, the need to combat the crisis would dominate policy decisions. For instance, the credit crisis period evidently required, for quite a while, a laser-like focus by the Committee on market stability and functioning. Success in containing a crisis, which might entail policies more or less unthinkable in more normal times, would be required for the Fed's dual mandate again to assume its central place in deliberations—not that it is ever really out of sight or mind. Questions related more specifically to the Fed's unusual policy strategies in the two major postwar crises are discussed in chapter 7.

While Committee members clearly determine policy based on their own judgments, it appears that the staff's economic forecast is a major background influence on the Committee's thinking—that is nearly inevitable, considering the thoroughness in the forecast's preparation and the history of ongoing, interactive discussions from meeting to meeting that frame and influence the thinking processes of both Committee members and the staff.

In the end, the Committee's policy judgment depends not only on its view about the strength or weakness of the economy but also, of course, as continually noted in this book, on their view of the potential for inflation, their principal target over the long run. In that respect, their assessment appears to depend to a great extent on the so-called output gap, which represents the extent to which the nation's actual output (represented by real GDP) is above or below what the nation can produce at something like maximum employment.

When the economy is running well below its potential, there is considerable room for improvement in employment conditions, and inflation is viewed as a minor current problem, if one at all—the FOMC's apparent view of the economy over the first three and a half years of recovery from the deep crisis-induced recession. In line with that approach to policy, one can expect that as the output gap narrows and the unemployment rate drops significantly further, at some point inflation pressures will become more of an influence on policy; the Fed's dual economic objectives will, at a minimum, become more equally weighted. The odds on policy tightening will rise.

How do Committee members frame and communicate their decision about policy?

The first and principal public communication of policy after an FOMC meeting is the short press release issued once the meeting is adjourned. It provides a rounded description of the policy just adopted. It contains the essence of operating directive provided to the account manager that day—the funds rate objective and other instructions affecting the government security market operations—as well as surrounding explanatory language related to the Committee's policy stance. The explanatory wording in the press release supplements the policy directive and completes the description of the FOMC's policy stance.

Indeed, the background language in recent years has been every bit as important as the policy directive and its federal funds rate target. It highlights recent economic and financial developments were main influences not only on the funds rate objective but also on other decisions implemented through the government securities market (such as, in recent years, long-term security purchases and the associated quantitative expansion of the Fed's balance sheet). Crucially, it also indicates factors the Committee will take into account in deciding on the duration of its current policy stance and provides information about current expectations. For instance, in the last meeting of 2012, the FOMC for the first time introduced specific thresholds for evaluating the potential duration of its current Federal funds rate policy rather than simply providing date-based guidance.

The thresholds were based on the Fed's dual objectives. To quote from the press release following the meeting, "the Committee decided to keep the target range for the federal funds at 0 to 1/4 percent and currently anticipates that this exceptionally low range for the federal funds rate will be appropriate at least as long as the unemployment rate remains above 6-1/2 percent, inflation between one and two years ahead is projected to be no more than a half percentage point above the Committee's 2 percent longer-run goal, and longer-term inflation expectations continue to be well-anchored." A few other related conditions, including financial developments, follow that provide, in good central banking tradition, even additional room for interpretation, judgment, and freedom of policy action.

It cannot be known at this time whether this is a temporary approach to provide better guidance to markets in light of the continued uncertainty about when the FOMC will begin a return to more normal operations following these recent long crises and postcrises years when the funds rate has been frozen near zero and the Fed's balance sheet and the nation's monetary base have ballooned. Once that passes, in a more normal period, it might seem complex and confusing to keep altering price and employment thresholds, especially in small increments as the economy evolves. It could risk looking too much like an excess of fine-tuning and possibly puzzle rather than reassure markets. The contentious questions about the practical priority between the Committee's two fundamental employment and inflation objectives that are implicit in the approach will become more obvious once the employment objective no longer dominates policy thinking.

Still, providing guidance of some sort about future policy adjustments, no matter how tenuous or surrounded by caveats, seems more in line with how financial markets and businesses view the world. Both price their products and form their plans with one eye on current conditions but with the other, very wary, eye on the future.

Economic difficulties to a great extent are rooted in misjudgments about the future—for instance, in the formation of expectations about the overall economic outlook by businesses that lead them either to over- or underinvest in capital equipment, or judgments by borrowers and investors that lead them either to become ebullient and risk being caught overextended or to remain too fearful and hold the economy back. And for the Fed especially, there is always the overriding problem of assuring the public and markets that it is doing all it can to keep the real economy moving along without also arousing inflation expectations and all the difficulties they entail for smooth implementation of policy.

These problems are compounded by the fact that monetary policy works with a lag, uncertain as its length may be. Policy actions today impact the economy over time, with peak effects often several months away. So indications about the Fed's attitude toward the future are important to private markets and businesses. In recent years, Fed intentions have become more frequently and more clearly revealed, but businesses and markets are, nevertheless, still left with an unavoidable uncertainty. They can be pretty sure, based on historical experience that the Fed's current judgments about policy strategy will inevitably change, and neither they nor the Fed can be sure when.

The minutes released two weeks following an FOMC meeting provide further detail about the discussion and are a further effort toward clarifying the policy stance as quickly as possible. They have, on occasion, led to further market adjustments as the public changed its perception of policy's intent, such as when the minutes showed that support for a particular policy move was less strongly held than the market had expected.

In addition, the chairman has recently initiated televised press conferences, held four times per year right after the decision has been announced, where he responds to questions and may provide additional background about the Committee's economic thinking and the policy adopted. They have so far taken place following those meetings at which the Summary of Economic Projections (SEP) and the associated projections of the funds rate have been formulated. Generally, they have been plain vanilla, free of surprises or subtle hints. Whatever shadings of the "consensus" view expressed at the meeting is contained in the official minutes released two weeks later.

How influential is the chairman in the policy votes?

The chairman's influence on policy votes depends in large part on his personality and the extent to which his policymaking colleagues hold him in respect—which in turn depends on his personal grasp of the issues, his fairness in running meetings, and, and perhaps most important, the extent to which he has gained public stature. I have personally watched and been quite close to five of the seven postwar chairmen starting with Martin through Volcker, but I take account of Greenspan and Bernanke mainly from an outsider's viewpoint.

As to a chairman's influence, my judgment would be that he is best viewed as, with an exception here and there, being worth at least one or maybe two additional votes in ordinary circumstances. It is his task to defend Committee decisions before Congress and the public, and, in that light, there is generally some willingness to bend in his direction, provided he is not too far ahead or behind the Committee as a whole.

A chairman should know that, and he will generally be astute enough not to put himself in such a position. But to retain the respect that assures him of an extra vote or two, he needs to be perceived as an interested leader willing to take a position, and not one who merely sits and searches for consensus—too passive a chairman will lose respect. It's a fine line he walks.

When it comes to a major paradigm shift in how policy is carried out, I would say that it could not be accomplished without a chairman's clear leadership. This can be seen in the two great postwar crisis periods through the implementation of an ultimately successful new approach to policy in the battle against inflation in the early 1980s and the Fed's effectiveness in quickly bringing together its various institutional capabilities to contain the worst of the recent credit crisis.

Inflation would not have been controlled the way it was without implementation of Volcker's innovative proposal; it would not have been done without his push. Somewhat similar proposals were considered in the 1970s, but Burns, chairman at the time, did not favor those approaches, and they died in one way or another, such as in a subcommittee's inability to make them convincingly operational.

From my outside perspective, I would judge that the Fed's successful efforts to contain the credit crisis, unique in its history, must have depended largely on Bernanke's leadership. Once the crisis was clearly and unfortunately threatening to get out of hand, he seemed promptly to realize what had to be done and set about organizing to do so. Given the central role of the chairman in coordinating the system-wide effort required, his own energy and leadership appeared crucial.

Why has the Fed become much more open about policy in recent decades?

It appears that changing times and attitudes in the country have led the Fed to become more open in recent years. The public has become less and less tolerant of secrecy on the part of elected decision-makers and their appointees—both here and more widely around the world. The more developed countries are at the forefront of the issue; although, the idea of transparency is beginning to seep into public consciousness in less developed, less democratic countries.

This changing trend was reflected legislatively here in the latter part of the 1960s in the Freedom of Information Act (FOIA) passed during the Johnson presidency. It was amended in the mid-1970s under Ford, pretty much creating the basic FOIA now in force (though with a number of further amendments over subsequent years). Exemptions—such as those related to national security, breaches of privacy, endangering the stability of a particular financial institution—exist of course. The Fed, especially its monetary policy process, was exempt in a number of ways. For instance, meetings of the FOMC were closed to the public, though meetings to decide on bank and other regulations for which the Fed was responsible were to be open to the public.

Over time, with public and congressional pressures for information pertaining to policy becoming more urgently felt, the FOMC gradually became more open, more prompt, and eventually more specific in its communications. Not all this was in response to political pressures and changes in the social and cultural environment. Among central bankers and a number of economic specialists in the monetary policy field (some of whom have become heads of central banks), more open communication of policy objectives and background thinking began to seem advantageous for policy effectiveness.

At least judging from practice in the United States, it appears that policymakers now believe that the more the public and markets know about a central banks' immediate policy objectives and associated strategy for implementing policy into the future, the better the odds on an effective monetary policy. In a sense, this approach could be viewed as in a way heralded under Volcker's chairmanship, when the Fed publicly proclaimed a paradigmatic shift in policy in the fall of 1979 that was intended to remain in place at least until the damaging inflation of the period came under control.

Volcker effectively used the chairman's bully pulpit to convince markets, businesses, and labor that the Fed would stick to the policy. Nonetheless, the tactical steps by the FOMC in implementing policy meeting by meeting remained closely held and were revealed only in the process of policy operations in the market. In those days, the parameters of the FOMC's actual decision at one meeting were not released to the public until after the following meeting had taken place.

The Fed became increasingly open about its thinking and policy plans beginning under Greenspan, in the last dozen or so years of the twentieth century and first few years of the twenty-first century, and went much further under his successor, Bernanke. Originally appointed as chairman by President Bush in 2006 and reappointed by President Obama in 2010, Bernanke represents a generational shift in leadership at the Fed and in professional economic training (having been a leading monetary economist in his distinguished academic career). Under him, the institution has laid out its thinking about prospective policy and key economic developments with increasing frequency and detail, as already described.

Still, as of this writing, the Committee has not found a way to put together something like a single consensus economic projection by members and a related single consensus federal funds rate projection—by no means an easy task in practice and not even clearly desirable. The economic future is inherently fuzzy—always has been—so that a degree of looseness and uncertainty in the Committee's outlook is probably a better reflection of the reality it deals with.

Even so, all this information can be both revealing and confusing. It is necessarily contingent; that is, it can change on a dime when economic conditions in the real world do not cooperate, as is often their wont. So how seriously the markets and the business community should take any one set of projections is always open to question. Also, the forecasts and discussion in the minutes are anonymous, so that it is impossible to differentiate the more influential members' opinions, like that of the chairman, from others.

Can there be too much openness?

It's not so much a question of communicating to the public too much or too little about the Committee's policy decision. It is more a problem of ensuring that the decisions made do not lead to counterproductive misinterpretation by the market and the public.

There are no problems I can see from making the guidelines for current policy operations perfectly clear, and the clearer the better. For instance, announcement of a specific federal funds rate target for operations is an improvement on the ambiguity inherent in characterizing the target as money market conditions with all the adjectival modifiers required, such as unchanged, slightly tighter/easier, somewhat tighter/easier.

If there were to be a problem, it would seem to come from possible unanticipated market reactions to indications about future policy. Experience in the Greenspan and Bernanke periods is illustrative of issues in that respect.

Under Greenspan, the Fed, by sharply lowering the federal funds rate did its part in stimulating economic recovery from the recession that followed the sharp drop in the stock market in 2000. But a problem, more evident in retrospect than prospect, came when the Fed kept the rate very low (even at times negative in real terms as earlier mentioned) as the economy began to recover. More importantly, however, the FOMC announced in its postmeeting policy statements that it intended to leave the rate low for an extended period. And when, after some while, the Fed began to raise the rate, it announced in effect that future rate increases would be quite gradual.

While the Greenspan Fed signaled its rate intentions to the market because it was uncertain about the pace of recovery and had a lingering fear of actual price deflation, the unanticipated result was to encourage markets to act on a belief that lastingly cheap short-term credit was available to finance investments in longer-term assets. This helped launch the unfortunate housing boom with homebuyers lured in over their head by cheap variable rate mortgages. More generally, the prospect of sustained low cost short-term borrowing made it psychologically too easy (by smoothing away an edge of uncertainty) for financial institutions and other allegedly sophisticated investors to indulge in the widespread excess leverage that cut across major markets and became a fundamental cause of the severity of the credit crisis.

The Bernanke Fed too signaled its intentions to hold the federal funds rate down over a sustained period early on in the credit crisis period. Indeed, it has been close to zero for about four years as of this writing (the beginning of 2013) and the latest Fed projections suggest a few more years to go. Assuring markets that the funds rate would remain low into the future signaled an extended period of monetary ease partly to make it very clear that there would be more than ample liquidity as the economy attempted to recover from the crisis.

That seems to have been a very useful approach in the awful economic circumstances of the period. But, as it turned out, much more was required of the Fed, which was left holding the policy bag once fiscal policy failed to follow through. The assurance that the funds rate would remain at zero was then combined with the policy of expanding the Fed's balance sheet through purchases of longer-term securities. In the end, the zero funds rate became so intimately tied into a policy of quantitative easing that it is difficult to distinguish it as a policy instrument by itself. In any event, I would say that thus far it has done some good and no harm.

The Greenspan and Bernanke Feds' contrasting experiences with providing such clear signals of the Fed's future monetary policy stance to the market—always subject to change of course—do leave lingering questions about the desirability of that approach. Additional practical experience perhaps will help tip the balance one way or another. But I doubt anything very clear will emerge. It obviously depends on the circumstances and a matter of judgment.

One might also raise questions about too much openness with official economic forecasts into the future. They too bear some risk if they end up misleading markets into actions that are counterproductive for society. A weak forecast, say, that persuades businesses to hold back on spending and causes the economy to be even weaker than anticipated, or not as strong as it might otherwise have been, would be one. Somehow, I doubt economic forecasts, in contrast to policy actions, have such power. Free markets do have their own inner dynamic that runs along independently of forecasts. The economy is not likely to be confined by the Fed's statistical projections if its inner dynamic is profitably set on a different course. Policy promises may be one thing; statistical forecasts are another less powerful one.

Anyhow, I feel assured by an opinion that I associate—in my memory from earlier years at the Fed—with a high-placed official who was rather allergic to economic forecasts, though their day had by then come as an aid for shaping policy discussions. In a none too serious off-the-cuff discussion, I heard, among other things, the view that if you must forecast, then forecast either rarely or frequently.

If rarely, they will soon be forgotten. If frequently, the importance of individual forecasts will diminish, and, as time goes on, one's track record will become confused enough not to be remembered. Thus, over time, forecasts will fade into irrelevance.

6

THE FED'S ROLE, OTHER DOMESTIC POLICIES, AND CONDITIONS ABROAD

What policies outside the Fed's control most influence its policy effectiveness?

With regard to policies that are, like the Fed's monetary policy, aimed at influencing the economy as a whole, the federal government's fiscal policy would be at the top of the list. Fiscal policy does not have the unique power to control inflation that the Fed has, but it can help stimulate economic growth, sometimes more effectively than monetary policy. The Fed's influence on the country's spending is indirect through its effects on liquidity and interest rates, but fiscal policy's influence is more direct through taxation and spending decisions of the government that affect jobs and the amount of income available for spending or saving.

Coordination of fiscal and monetary policies has long been viewed as a key policy issue for the nation, in particular since the influential economic analysis of the British economist, John Maynard Keynes, in the 1930s highlighted the importance of fiscal policy in promoting recovery from depressions. Indeed, one of the main purposes behind the semiannual monetary policy report that the Fed makes to both houses of Congress—which originated from a law passed in the late 1970s at a time when inflation had been too high and growth too low (stagflation)—was to determine how well monetary policies were being coordinated with other governmental policies in the interests of a fully employed economy as well as inflation control. That particular law, the Full Employment and Balance Growth Act, is no longer on the books.

Most recently, in the wake of the credit crisis, regulatory policies have come to the fore as another area that can affect monetary policy effectiveness and require coordinated efforts. Since the Fed is an important player in the regulatory area and was founded in large part to make sure that problems in banking markets would not lead to major financial crises, those issues come very close to home.

Because of its own perceived regulatory laxness, the Fed has been viewed both as a contributor to the credit crisis (along with other regulatory agencies) as well as the institution that has been crucial and successful in keeping the crisis contained. How to achieve a better and workable integration of regulatory and monetary policies is by no means simple and is still a work in progress.

The government's other numerous domestic policy responsibilities—such as those influencing labor markets, business practices, consumer credit, fair trade, tariffs and the like—can have indirect effects on monetary policy but are not as central as fiscal and regulatory policies to the Fed's principal goals of maximum employment, minimum inflation, and avoidance of destabilizing financial crises. Nonetheless, it does remain the case that certain other governmental policies, for instance those that do not sufficiently encourage flexibility in labor markets or competitiveness in pricing decisions, can make the Fed's efforts to attain its dual economic mandate more practically difficult.

Policies abroad and associated economic conditions had long seemed only distantly related to the Fed's policy decisions. As has become increasingly evident in recent decades, however, the distance is growing shorter. The United States' share of world output has been on a slow but fairly steady decline from the country's unusual dominance in the special circumstances of the immediate postwar period. That trend continues in today's world, as the productive potential of modern technology and of more competitive and enterprise-oriented economies have become more widely known through the ease and speed of modern communication and more widespread education—not to mention the natural desire of people all over the world to raise their standard of living as the opportunities become known.

Thus, the Federal Reserve now has more of a need than before to take account of policies and conditions abroad in framing its approach. Nonetheless, its ability to pursue an independent monetary policy based on U.S. economic conditions and interests does not yet appear to have been seriously eroded, given the basic economic strength of the country. Despite recent major financial problems, the role of the dollar and of the nation's financial markets in the international financial arena remains almost uniquely strong, if not quite as unparalleled as earlier. It has been buoyed by the enormous liquidity and breadth of U.S. markets.

Also, while the exchange value of the dollar inevitably fluctuates in response to underlying economic and financial conditions, confidence in dollar markets as a secure place to do business has been buttressed by a sense of safety and operational reliability embedded in the stable political, legal, and regulatory environment that has traditionally surrounded them. That is not so very different from markets in other major developed countries or areas. But it will take considerable time for markets in large emerging economies, such as China and Brazil, to be viewed with a similar level of confidence by global investors.

How do fiscal and monetary policies best fit together?

It depends on circumstances. There is no simple trade-off between the two policies, given their varying effects on the economy. It is not just that a more expansive fiscal policy may require a tighter monetary policy, and tighter fiscal policy an easier monetary policy—though that can often be the case.

Rather, it is particularly important to coordinate the policies in a supportive way so that major economic problems can be more readily resolved. Issues of mutual support between fiscal and monetary policies become most evident when the real economy is near its extremes of either weakness (with unemployment unusually high) or strength (when employment is near its maximum and inflation a major threat).

As indicated in earlier chapters of this book, monetary policy is more effective at restraining inflation, and containing a credit crisis, than it is at speeding up economic growth in a weak economy performing below its potential. It has a direct effect on inflation by restraining the liquidity and credit that feed it and on a credit crisis by in effect replacing bad market credits with its own good ones. But it stimulates spending more indirectly; how much spending is generated depends on how sensitive borrowers and spenders are to the greater liquidity and lower interest rates that are monetary policy's stock in trade.

In depressions or serious recessions that follow major financial crises, monetary policy's success in stimulating the economy is often constrained by the huge shock to confidence suffered by businesses and consumers, which makes them unusually fearful of borrowing and spending beyond what they view as a minimum at that point. With future prospects looking glum indeed, they simply hold back as much as possible almost no matter how low interest rates get. Their responsiveness to more credit, greater liquidity, and lower interest rates is greatly reduced. In addition, lending institutions, those that have survived the traumatic crisis, become increasingly wary of making loans and require a long period to regain their footing and nerve.

As one example, monetary policy did not revive the economy in any significant way after the stock market crash and banking crisis that led to the very deep and lasting 1930s depression. At that time, it was not only because the market participants were too shell-shocked to be sufficiently responsive to the Fed's easing efforts. It was also because policymakers in those days—though admittedly using monetary instruments more technically limited than now (by various collateral requirements for instance)—still did not seem to recognize how strongly expansive a monetary policy was required in such drastic conditions to make any dent at all.

With such an unfortunate precedent in mind and given the subsequent advances in economic understanding and instrumental flexibility, the Fed has done a much better job following the highly threatening credit crisis of 2008–2009. The crisis was followed by a recession that was bad but hardly comparable to the extreme unemployment, pervasive bread lines, and other economic and social disasters of the earlier depression. Nonetheless, the ensuing recovery has been discouragingly slow and social disruptions not easily repaired.

What was missing in both cases was adequately supportive use of the other major macro-economic tool, fiscal policy. Situations in which monetary policy instruments are unable to provide sufficient impetus to the economy—either because public confidence in the future is so badly shaken or because there is already so much liquidity in the economy that even more can have no further significant positive impact on the public's willingness to borrow and spend (often termed a liquidity trap)—are precisely the times when fiscal policy is most required to step in.

Unlike monetary policy instruments, the instruments of fiscal policy—governmental outlays and taxation powers— have a more direct and certain impact on the nation's total spending and the private sector's income. An expansive fiscal policy, via increased government spending or lower taxes, will initially and directly raise the nation's real GDP and disposable income, as well as the country's budgetary deficit of course. The knock-on effects from that initial action as the new spending ripples through goods and services markets (termed multiplier effects in the economic literature) will help bolster confidence and stimulate some further lending and borrowing activity that monetary policy alone could not accomplish. Jobs and income will rise more than they would have otherwise.

The healthier the underlying economy, the less powerful and lasting the fiscal stimulus need be. History unfortunately suggests that some crises are so pervasive and shockingly unexpected as to leave a country in a very weak state psychologically. In those circumstances, it may take a stronger and longer fiscal stimulus to help create the job and income growth that is fundamental to restoring confidence in the economy. Policy economics being as much an art as a science, it is very hard to judge in advance.

In any event, as an economy regains strength and confidence, the need for an actively expansive fiscal policy to support an expansive monetary policy fades. The budget deficits that helped spur the economy will begin to retreat on their own, as tax collections rise. But more of a retreat may turn out to be needed for both economic and social reasons.

Politicians, the ultimate arbiters of fiscal policy, will be faced, as they always are, with finding a balance between federal taxation policies and governmental outlays that not only fit well with macro-economic conditions but also satisfy canons of fairness and equity in our open, democratic, enterprise-driven society. Monetary policy in practice would have to adapt. In that context, the simple trade-off idea that an easier fiscal policy might require a tighter monetary policy (and a tighter one an easier monetary policy) would begin to be of more practical importance.

As a crude rule of thumb (to illustrate the issues involved) one might take the view that a balanced federal budget could be viewed as a desirable goal when the economy is at or nearing its maximum level of employment. (That, of course, raises serious political questions about the extent to which the government should be directly involved in society's life—i.e., about whether balance should involve more or less federal outlays and more or less offsetting tax collections.) If fiscal policy were instead more expansive, with significant budgetary deficits when the economy was producing at or near its potential, it would pose a dilemma for monetary policy and also prove counterproductive for the economy's longer-run growth and efficiency.

Under such circumstances, because the government is not as sensitive as private borrowers to changing credit conditions, longer-term market interest rates are likely to rise, quite possibly to the point of squeezing out productive capital spending by businesses as the government issues more debt to pay for its added spending or new tax cuts. Such a displacement of private capital spending, especially if prolonged, would, through adverse long-run effects on U.S. productivity and our competitive position in the international world, begin to limit the capacity for domestic economic growth and job creation.

Upward pressure on interest rates would be even more pronounced if the Fed felt the need to tighten another notch to assure that the new debt issued by the government, with the economy already at or near its potential, was not in effect monetized and inflationary and that market expectations of inflation were not unduly further aroused. That would then add the risk of a transitional recession to the potential structural problems for the economy from adding fiscal deficits to an economy already at or near its potential.

In general, the best fit between fiscal and monetary policies depends on what the economy needs to keep growth on a stable course. In a very weak economy, a counter-cyclical fiscal policy may have a stronger hand to play than monetary policy no matter how easy it gets. But when an economy is approaching its potential and the Fed is focused on keeping inflation and inflation expectations under control, monetary policy will work better, and with less market complications, when fiscal policy is at least effectively neutral or supportively on the tight side of its norm.

In the long more normal periods of time between an extremely weak and a quite strong economy, when economic growth is chugging along satisfactorily with no more than its usual ups and downs, fiscal policy can be viewed by the Fed not so much as an alternative macro-economic policy whose help one way or another would be much appreciated. Rather, it can be taken, and in practice necessarily is taken, as simply one among the many other factors in the economy that influence real economic growth and the demands for credit and liquidity in the nation—and thereby, depending on the overall economic outlook, the stance of monetary policy. The Fed's basic projections of real GDP and inflation simply assume a particular governmental fiscal stance, based on tax and spending programs currently in place. In that way, the two policies are fit together, even though the Fed at times might believe that a somewhat different balance would make life easier.

How are decisions about coordinate roles for fiscal and monetary policies made in practice?

The most accurate answer would seem to be: catch as catch can. There is no single authority in the United States that has the power to make such a decision. The Fed is authorized to make monetary policy. The administration influences fiscal policy through tax and spending recommendations to the Congress, where ultimate authority lies (subject to Presidential veto power). The government's budget balance, whether a surplus, deficit, or neutral, embodies the country's fiscal policy.

Yet it is far from clear whether or to what extent the budgetary process in any given year has been determined by an overriding view about some need to adjust the stance of fiscal policy as a macro-economic tool to better fit with evolving economic conditions. In general, it seems assumed that monetary policy would adapt as needed to ensure that the government's budgetary policies do not upset the economy.

In the course of a year, however, as economic conditions change, fiscal policy adjustments may be undertaken for one macro-economic reason or another—and coordination with monetary policy sometimes raising contentious issues. In 1968, to go back to a time when there was a great belief in trade-offs between the two policies, the government pushed for a tax increase. Once enacted, the Fed responded by lowering the discount rate, a classical coordination move to avoid any excessive weakening of the economy—one apparently supported by the Board chairman at the time but only reluctantly within the Fed system. About a year later, the rate drop had to be reversed because the economy had not weakened as had been feared by some.

In a later period, early in the Reagan years, a large three-stage tax decrease was adopted. No trade-off had apparently been agreed to. The Fed was busy bringing the great inflation under control at the time, with a rather strong recession in its wake. Early in the decade, a substantial economic recovery began; the lower tax rates (some fairly soon reversed) began to seem out of phase with the need for monetary policy to keep inflation down while the recovery was gathering its own momentum.

So the practical ability to adapt fiscal actions on a reasonably timely basis to ongoing changes in the economic outlook as promptly as desired would require a very cooperative Congress (which is iffy at best, especially in recent years) and better foresight than usual in these matters. To provide the administration with a fiscal weapon that could be wielded rather promptly to encourage real GDP growth in a weak economy, for instance, the idea of a shelf of public works deliberately stocked for that purpose had been bruited about in much earlier decades, when Keynesian economics was more in favor and the Great Depression more a part of people's experience. That idea never got very far. Indeed, even what might seem to be a remote cousin, the notion raised in the early days of the Obama administration of shovel-ready public works that could be funded and effective action taken quickly proved rather illusory because of various bureaucratic and other problems.

Nonetheless, there is always some built-in budgetary flexibility through which fiscal policy can make a positive contribution during a recession. In periods of declining employment and general business, government tax collections also drop and the federal budget goes into deficit as ongoing federal outlays continue and some, like unemployment compensation and other sorts of aid to help ease poverty, actually rise.

While this growing fiscal deficit cushions an economic decline, it may well not be proactive enough to help turn it around. Nor, incidentally, should it be viewed as indicative of how large a claim the federal government is making on the nation's resources over the long-run. That is much better shown by estimates of the government's budgetary position when real GDP is at or around its potential—that is, when it is not influenced by transitory effects of the automatic economic stabilizers built into the budget that move it toward deficit in a recession and away in recovery. (Such a measure has at various times been known as a "high employment deficit," or "structural deficit," or simply described as a cyclically adjusted budget.)

Apart from these built-in stabilizers, it takes time to provide added fiscal support to a struggling economy. There are time lags before a need is recognized by the powers that be, more lags in the process of political negotiation, and finally the lag in implementation as needed bureaucratic processes are worked through. When finally all is in place, economic conditions may have changed considerably. At that point it will be up to the Fed to make the necessary policy adjustment to help keep economic growth on a sustainable course.

In the end, then, monetary policy becomes the coordinator of last resort. And it can perform only as well as the unique powers of its policy instruments permit.

How do regulatory issues relate to monetary policy and its dual economic objectives?

The connection between the Fed's use of its regulatory and supervisory authority over banks (and related institutions) and the process of implementing monetary policy to achieve its basic dual economic objectives of maximum employment and price stability can be described as complementary. Unfortunately, however, there was not much evidence before the crisis of due diligence in assuring that they were continuously as compatible as one might like. After the credit crisis, a more closely monitored or integrated connection has obviously come to seem desirable, though how practically possible remains an open question.

The Fed's regulatory and supervisory functions are basically aimed at keeping the banking system safe and sound through good and bad economic times. This is accomplished through use of the tools of the regulatory trade—such as regulations presumably adapted as needed to changes in financial technology and practice governing various specific banking activities; the supervisory examination of banking organizations under the Fed's jurisdiction to verify adherence to regulations and the law; and, subsequent to passage of the DFA, special oversight over large bank holding companies and large nonbank financial institutions.

The instruments of monetary policy, by contrast, are aimed at influencing the nation's overall monetary and credit conditions to sustain economic growth and keep inflation under control. In that process, they are continuously adjusted and policymakers have to be prepared to turn on a dime as economic news unlooses its dose of surprises. The Fed's regulatory processes, however, unfold in what might be called a more deliberate manner. They deal with ongoing complex competitive business and customer relationships and also have a clear need to coordinate regulations and supervisory emphases with other similar institutions (here and abroad) or make the attempt to do so.

In brief, the regulatory process is not at all like policy formulation at the FOMC, where clear decisions are made about once every six weeks. To be a bit fanciful, it is more like a never-ending nationwide or worldwide meeting with large numbers of official participants coming and going as the markets continue on their innovative ways. An announcement is made as changing conditions may require. If the job of regulatory officials has been well accomplished, it will help ensure that monetary and other governmental policies can be implemented smoothly and economic activities and the financing of them can rest on a sound fundament.

But it remains difficult for regulatory adjustments and monetary policy actions to be well tuned together in adapting to, for instance, cyclical variations in economic activity. Perhaps, certain regulatory actions might be timed to help monetary policy along at critical economic junctures. One possibility would be if efforts were made to raise capital requirements on banks (or certain segments of the banking system) as a way of restraining potential lending excesses in coordination with a monetary policy decision.

Under some circumstances, such an action might forestall a full-scale monetary tightening that might otherwise needlessly affect markets across the board. That would most easily be carried out if the Fed had control of both policies. However, their control of regulatory matters affecting capital requirements at all banks as well as bank holding companies cannot in practice be readily exercised without taking account of impacts on other institutions and the viewpoint of other regulators with whom their authority may overlap. The timing might or might not turn out to be workable.

But then there are instances, fortunately not very common, where the feedback between regulatory policies and the needs of monetary policy can be quite negative. It is not hard to think of actual occasions like that. The most obvious would be a failure by regulators to be adequately diligent in face of newly evolving and potentially undesirable market practices.

The weakness in supervision of lending practices (perhaps customer suitability for one) leading up to the recent mortgage crisis was, as it turned out, an unfortunate instance, and so was the passivity of authorities in face of unusually pervasive and heavy leveraging across all markets at the same time. Regulatory laxness in these circumstances tended to weaken the financial fundament, and it cracked under enormous stress.

When it does, the Fed's discount window can become the primary instrument of monetary policy. It can be employed to make loans to institutions or markets in trouble. When used on a small-scale while markets as a whole are quite functional, monetary policy can be implemented in a relatively normal way. But if, as in 2008–2009, for a combination of reasons markets start threatening to become broadly dysfunctional, discount window usage will overwhelm usual policy approaches as the Fed turns its full and undivided attention to restoring some sense of stability to finance. Its balance sheet becomes distorted far from its norm as the Fed's lending function in effect replaces the credit that the market is no longer able or willing to provide.

In those conditions, the skills and experience of financial analysts and staff engaged in supervisory and regulatory activities at the Fed then become more broadly useful by helping to examine the portfolios of borrowing institutions, some of which may be in emergency situations. At that time, questions about valuation of collateral also become particularly important, as do related questions about haircut requirements; that is, how much will the Fed lend against particular classes of collateral. Such administrative cooperation among areas of the Fed system can have positive side effects; they can be helpful by leading to better practical understanding and appreciation of the coordinate importance of both regulatory and monetary questions throughout the Fed system as a whole and how they may impinge on one another.

How does the Fed's own regulatory authority fit into the nation's regulatory structure?

The nation's financial regulatory structure is complex and overlapping. Our political system entails involvement of not only both federal and state authorities but also overlapping federal agencies' jurisdictions, especially those connected to banking.

The Fed is a major player in the regulation and supervision of banking organizations, probably the major player. It directly regulates and supervises bank holding companies and state-chartered member banks. It shares regulatory responsibilities for activities of national banks with the Office of the Comptroller of the Currency (OCC), a bureau of the U.S. Treasury and the chartering authority of those banks. And it is solely responsible for regulatory oversight of foreign branches of all member banks, whether state or nationally chartered, as well as of certain other international banking activities including those of foreign banks in the United States. The Federal Deposit Insurance Company (FDIC) also has an oversight responsibility over all insured banks to evaluate their suitability for deposit insurance.

This diverse group of regulators and supervisors is the product of our nation's historical development and of a philosophy that has attempted to balance local and national interests, as well as differing national interests. The regulators are continuously confronted by a need to negotiate reasonably consistent positions to guide examiners and supervisors of the various institutions in the midst of market changes that do not let up, especially in recent decades. They have had to take account of a rapid pace of market integration across states and, internationally, across borders. Latterly, more consideration has had to be given to the increased intermingling of traditional banking activities with other (more speculative, or risky) financial services in judging the condition of banking organizations.

As one might imagine, over time, agreements are reached and modified as circumstances change. A financial institutions examination council, comprising top officials of the various bank regulatory agencies, has long existed to coordinate activities and establish uniform standards for examination and supervision of the various depository institutions and to maintain contact with state regulators. However, agreements and contacts are one thing. Practice is another. There is always some room for differences in emphasis in bank examination procedures and regulatory enforcement depending on the amount of resources available to the particular agency, how strongly the agency head may feel about one area or another, or similar bureaucratic-type issues that inevitably arise, even in monolithic institutions, and become more of a factor where power centers with competing interests and some independence of authority are involved.

The general point is that the regulatory independence of the Fed and its speed of action are greatly limited by its role as only one among others within the country's regulatory structure, even though it may be the most influential and powerful one in the banking area. In recent decades, however, banking has become far from an island unto itself. It never quite was, of course, even though in the wake of the Great Depression Congress passed what is termed the Glass-Steagall Act that separated old-style commercial banking (e.g., deposit-taking and customer-oriented lending) from much of the presumed riskier securities-type business to make banks safer for the public—although in practice the deposit insurance passed at the same time was probably just as, if not more, effective.

However, as the postwar period progressed, the structure of finance began to change almost beyond recognition as a result of cultural, institutional, and technological developments; the purely commercial and deposit-taking banks were looking outdated and were being out-competed. In reflection, laws changed and administrative interpretations gradually became more liberal. Banks in the United States have now become much more intermeshed in broader securities markets than had probably ever been envisioned by Messrs. Glass and Steagall.

Banks are now associated, through bank holding companies, with a wide variety of financial activities. The Gramm-
Leach-Bliley Act of 1999, in particular, finally pretty much did
away in practice with the depression-era restrictions; it explicitly permitted a bank holding company to qualify as a financial
holding company that could undertake such activities as securities underwriting and dealing and merchant banking.

The original Bank Holding Company Act (initially passed
in 1956) made the Fed primarily responsible for regulating,
supervising, and approving activities that could be undertaken within a bank holding company. That brought Fed regulatory authority well beyond the traditional boundaries of
commercial banking and also into some potential conflict with
attitudes of affiliates' or subsidiaries' primary functional regulators (such as the SEC in the case of a broker-dealer). Some
have thought that the Fed employed its enhanced regulatory
powers in this area with too light a hand. If so, one can wonder
whether or how that may change in the new seemingly more
severe post-crisis atmosphere, and how that will be received
by the primary regulators of businesses involved.[1]

How has the Dodd-Frank Act influenced the
Fed's regulatory stance?

How much flexibility now exists for the Fed's regulatory
authority to be adapted as needed to support a current monetary policy also has to take account of the many changes
wrought by the DFA. That Act seems to encourage the Fed to
be more aggressive in its use of regulatory tools as the economic outlook shifts, at one point suggesting that adjustments
in bank capital requirements should take account of cyclical
economic conditions. The provision for one governor to be
appointed as vice chairman for supervision also signals a need
for continuing special attention to regulatory issues.

While something of a grab bag, the DFA was mainly concerned with ensuring that the dimensions of the 2008–2009

credit crisis did not recur. It established the Financial Stability Oversight Council with ten voting members (heads of the leading regulatory agencies and the U.S. Treasury) and five nonvoting ones. The Council is basically under control of the administration because a positive vote is effective only if it includes the Treasury.

With respect to the role of the Fed in connection with potential crises, the Act enhanced its regulatory powers over large bank holding companies (a minimum size of $50 billion initially set) and also gave it authority over certain large nonbank financial companies deemed to be systemically important. These were considered to be institutions that were threats to financial stability—that is, too big to fail. After due consultation with Council members and perhaps foreign regulators, the Fed is to set enhanced prudential standards, such as for risk-based capital and liquidity, for the institutions. They can be adjusted again as needed, one presumes, after due consultation.

Use of the discount window for emergency lending, a crucial monetary instrument for buffering the credit crisis of 2008–2009, was greatly altered by Dodd-Frank. The Fed is no longer permitted to make an emergency loan to help rescue a single specific firm in trouble, as had been the case with Bear Stearns in the spring of 2008; the failure to make an emergency loan to Lehman Brothers in September 2009 was the proximate cause of the second and disastrous phase of the crisis. Emergency loans are the only route through which nonmember banks (or expressed in a now more technically correct way, depository institutions not subject to the Fed's reserve requirements) and other institutions have access to the discount window.

A huge controversy arose about the Fed taking it upon itself to make emergency loans to avert failures that would risk seriously adverse market-wide repercussions. Many believed the loans would unduly encourage so-called moral hazard—that is, encourage others in the market to take undue risks because the down side would be limited by thoughts that the Fed would rescue them, with the ultimate cost (if any) being borne by the taxpayer.

That problem was recognized by Fed, so it would seem, and instances in which such loans were in fact made during the crisis were also approved by the U.S. Treasury, as indicated by its modest participation in the loans. This suggested governmental agreement that the loan was in the national interest. The potential cost was considered by the government to be offset by the gain in overall financial stability—a fair enough requirement for such controversial loans since they enter into the territory of political judgments that are the province of the government, not the Fed.

The DFA now limits emergency lending by the Fed to a "program or facility with broad-based eligibility," designed for last resort liquidity assistance and not structured to assist a specific firm. This would not seem very different at all from the programs under which the great bulk of lending during the crisis took place. Setting up such a program now by law specifically requires Treasury approval—which was not legally required by the previous law governing Fed emergency lending. Other provisions of the DFA provide rather complicated routes for governmental assistance to firms faced with actual bankruptcy as possible alternatives to normal bankruptcy procedures in the courts.

Whether these changes have or have not improved the Fed's ability to enhance financial stability through regulation and use of its discount window is not really knowable in advance. On the regulatory side, it has been given a better opportunity to act promptly to avert major troubles, through its authority over large banking and other financial institutions, but whether they will be recognized one can never be sure. And it will take time and strong convictions to act far enough in advance and work through coordination procedures with the Oversight Council to be as effective as one might hope. The worst of the recent credit crisis crashed upon us in such force not so much because public policy instruments were inadequate but because the potential for a really, really severe crisis was not recognized by monetary and regulatory policymakers almost up to the last minute; partly because of blinders embedded in the market, policy, and political cultures of the period; and partly because of the sheer, unadulterated difficulty of seeing the future before it arrives.

As to the emergency lending change, that would seem to remove a potentially potent weapon from the Fed; it will not have the ability to lend to a troubled nonmember institution facing financial difficulties unless it is made within a facility with broad-based eligibility for liquidity assistance. However, such an individual loan made promptly before an institution is viewed as bankrupt could be a crucial element in keeping a crisis from seriously worsening. The recent credit crisis was greatly intensified after the Fed decided not to lend to Lehman Brothers. It will never be known what would have happened if it had, but the DFA provisions, read literally, would not have given it the opportunity. They clearly suggest that the Congress does not favor such a loan.

Although occurring in much more stable times, a counter-example of a stabilizing individual loan made by the Fed (in cooperation with the FDIC), may be illustrative of what can be lost. In the 1980s, very large sums were loaned to a large member bank experiencing substantial deposit drains, partly caused by rumors about the deterioration in the quality of its assets—a liquidity crisis at an individual institution that would in due course raise the threat, if not the reality, of bankruptcy and cast doubt on other large institutions. The official loans kept the bank in business, though at considerable financial cost to shareholders and chief officers, until another large bank acquired it. This process helped defuse an iffy situation at the time.

The DFA provisions make it very difficult to implement such a solution for an individual nonmember institution suffering liquidity strains but not yet bankrupt; it would have no access to the discount window except as part of some broad-based emergency program. The Act seems to focus on provisions aimed more at providing liquidity to alleviate problems of getting through a crisis rather than promptly providing funds that might help avert them.

How might the Fed better integrate monetary and regulatory policies?

As mentioned before, spurred on by public and congressional discontent with the credit crisis and its aftermath, not to mention its own learning curve, the Fed seems to be in the process of evaluating this very question. From this outsider's perspective, it is a difficult one.

Regulatory and monetary policies have very different primary objectives—to restate, for regulatory policy, a safe and sound banking system, or more generally, a stable financial system; for monetary policy, essentially the dual economic objectives of stable prices and maximum employment. But they do clearly relate to each other since monetary policy instruments affect the economy through their influences on conditions in financial markets. The more stable and predictable are conditions in financial markets, the easier it is for monetary policy to focus on its fundamental economic objectives in employing its monetary instruments.

In general, monetary policy works best in viable financial markets free of serious systemic risks whether the economy is going through relatively good or relatively weak economic times. One might describe a systemic risk as involving the potential that the market as a whole will seriously break down and no longer be just a conduit for monetary policy (or even fulfill markets' basic function of distributing the nation's financial resources among savers and borrowers on a rational basis). Rather its behavior could so impair public confidence that the economy as a whole goes into a crisis mode that is not easily rectified by public policy.

The systemic health of the system is a matter of setting adequate prudential standards over a long period of time in negotiation with the many regulators involved here (and as needed abroad), and adjusting them as time goes on in light of market innovations and changing lender, borrower, and investor tastes and practices. Nowadays, because of the accelerated pace of change in finance and the ever-closer connections among expanding global markets, assessment of the potential for systemic risks afflicting a financial system is something of an ongoing process.

The Fed is just one among many regulators in this country, but it has a strong vested interest because of the crucial importance of monetary policy for the macro-economic welfare of the country. Thus, one would think that a regular public report from the Fed about the systemic health of the financial system would be an important guidepost in evaluating the potential for significant weak points, if any, that might be looming. Indeed, the DFA requires the new Fed vice chairman for supervision to report twice a year to Congress on the Fed's supervisory and regulatory activities. Presumably that could be extended to include a broader report on systemic health. Or one could be included in, or along with, the chairman's semiannual report on FOMC policy. The preparation and publication of such a report would increase the chances that regulatory actions could be more sensitively attuned to the monetary policy process.

But for a variety of institutional and other reasons, noted earlier, the Fed's regulatory authority cannot be considered anything like a flexible instrument of monetary policy in the same vein as, for example, open market operations. Even with added powers from the DFA, regulatory decisions normally involve a long process of negotiation with other domestic agencies with overlapping or related responsibilities, not to mention consideration of any international agreements on such things as prudential, capital, or liquidity standards of one sort or another. And now the Financial Stability Oversight Council has been added to the mix.

From that perspective, regulatory policies may be more suited to a longer-run structural role rather than a short-term policy role. They can and should help establish and maintain a banking and overall financial system that is fundamentally sound and at little risk of destabilizing crises.

However, so perfect a continuing financial world is something like a dream from a historical perspective. Crises, unpredicted and unexpected, seem to have been with us always. So circumstances may well arise in practice when it would be desirable to employ regulatory adjustments, such as in capital or liquidity standards, in a flexible, timely way to aid current monetary policy. That would fall under the authority of the Board of Governors, not the FOMC. To date, they have not been given much consideration, if any, as a useful complement to the Fed's usual monetary policy instruments. A closer and more fruitful connection between independent monetary policies and associated regulatory policies remains to be achieved.

How is Fed policy influenced by policies and conditions abroad?

Developments in the domestic economy are the dominant influence by far on the formulation of U.S. monetary policy. Economic conditions abroad have an indirect influence to the extent they affect our output, growth, and inflationary pressures. Projections of the nation's GDP necessarily take account of U.S. exports to foreign countries because they represent greater output here. Such forecasts also take account of imports from abroad because they can substitute for purchases of domestically produced goods and reduce our output. When exports exceed imports (a trade surplus), international conditions have a positive effect on our GDP and when imports exceed exports (a trade deficit) a negative effect.

Nonetheless, how the trade balance interacts with the domestic economy may in and of itself have some policy implications. If the economy is performing near its potential, a negative trade balance indicates that U.S. consumers and other domestic entities are spending beyond the nation's productive capacity and inflation is being contained by the availability of goods from abroad at highly competitive prices. That is not normally a sustainable situation. For instance, the dollar might begin to lose value in exchange markets and thereby put upward pressure on domestic prices as exporters seek to maintain their profit margins. The Fed might have to decide whether to tighten a bit sooner than otherwise to moderate total spending by domestic consumers and businesses and avert inflation before it gets too big a head of steam.

The problem becomes considerably more complicated when large trade deficits are continuing while the economy looks to be performing below its potential. This seemed to be a problem in the early years of this century, when China was running a huge trade surplus as a counterpart to a historically high U.S. trade deficit (relative to GDP). About twenty years or so earlier, there was a similar situation with Japan, at the time that country was making its dramatic inroads into world auto and technology markets.

In the more recent situation, there was much talk in markets and the press about unsustainable trade imbalances in the world economy, with the United States and China being the most notable. The large inflows of funds into this country from China (it was a time when that country bought massive amounts of U.S. government securities with its large foreign exchange earnings) helped fund the government's deficit and to an extent compensated for the exceptionally low personal saving rate at the time. It might also be argued that the availability of savings from abroad also could have, at the margin, facilitated the excess speculation that was heralding the credit crisis.

The Fed did not seem to let the international imbalances influence its monetary policy at all. It continued to be guided naturally enough at the time by what domestic economic conditions required with the economy still producing below its potential. With slack in our productive capacity, there seemed little reason to take monetary actions that might restrain domestic demand here and thus imports. Rather, it seemed more reasonable for China to rely less on exports as an engine of growth while also encouraging expansion of its own lagging domestic demand.

The foreign exchange and trade issues involved were, so it seemed, more properly tackled by intergovernmental negotiations, just as took place at the time of the initial Japanese surge into the international economy. As of this writing, China has for several years now very gradually been moving in those directions for its own domestic purposes.

The oil price shocks of the 1970s—one around mid-decade and the second late in the period—were another instance when international conditions had spillover effects on the domestic economy, this time much more noticeable and through their direct impact on inflationary pressures more definitely in the Fed's bailiwick. More so than they would now, the politically driven very large oil price hikes instigated by the oil-producing states of the Middle East had wide-ranging effects on other prices and the average level of prices in the United States.

Conceptually, a central bank has essentially two choices in the circumstances. It can through monetary expansion fully accommodate a one-time upward adjustment in the average level of prices, and then return to a normal policy aimed at reasonable price stability—with all the great uncertainties in getting from here to there and back to another here. Or it can through strong monetary restraint attempt to avert any significant lasting effect on the average level of prices, presumably at the cost of a very serious recession. The Fed of the day chose an in between course of gradually fending off the inflationary pressures, hoping to keep them from becoming seriously embedded in the economy and in domestic labor cost pressures. In the event, the average annual rate of inflation for the decade picked up notably, moderate recessions occurred, and growth on balance slowed.

Monetary policy chose the option that policymakers must have believed was most acceptable to the country, given the alternatives. In particular, too aggressive an approach would have probably caused a serious credit crisis in savings institutions, which at the time held mortgage assets with long maturities at fixed rates, financed by short-term deposits at relatively low ceiling rates. Widespread bankruptcies certainly loomed if depositors withdrew their funds in volume, or if ceiling rates had to be raised to keep pace with a sharp rise in shorter-term market rates implied by an even tighter monetary policy. In the event, the rather inevitable crisis in savings institutions (such as savings and loan associations and mutual savings banks) played itself out gradually under more flexible financial conditions in the 1980s.

In sum, the 1970s oil price crises were perhaps the most spectacular instance where foreign-driven events obviously had a powerful influence on the strategy of monetary policy, but the steps taken (among the evils available) were, of course, driven by purely domestic considerations. Whether the particular policy was the best possible has long been debated.

Will the Fed's ability to make monetary policy decisions on purely domestic grounds be significantly lessened by further integration of world financial markets?

Not for a long while I suspect. The dollar thus far remains the world's leading currency. It is acceptable worldwide, even under temporarily adverse circumstances here. The economy behind it is the largest in the world, and its financial markets are generally well regulated and subject to a consistent rule of law. As time goes on, no doubt the Chinese economy will outpace us in aggregate output though not per capita I tend to believe. When or whether its financial markets will develop the requisite legal, regulatory, and administrative structures for worldwide acceptability of its currency is open to question at this point.

The Euro is a currency area comparable to the dollar in size of its economy and sophistication of its financial institutions. But the deficiencies of its underlying institutional structure, with separate governments with their own fiscal and regulatory policies, have at the moment cast a little doubt on the general acceptability of the Euro outside its own borders—and even on how large and well integrated a currency area the Euro will turn out to be.

There seems little doubt, however, that the share of the U.S. economy in world economic output will continue to gradually diminish further from its postwar highs. It is easy to envision currency blocs eventually emerging that revolve around such economies as China, perhaps India, and perhaps Brazil, in addition to some sort of Euro zone and the United States. They would be large enough to adjust monetary policies mainly on purely domestic grounds. But they would also be large enough to have a significant influence on one another.

It is the smaller satellite countries around them that would not be in a position to pursue independent monetary policies. They would be in a position something like the smaller countries of Western Europe were before formation of the Euro zone. As capital flowed freely, the smaller countries of the zone could hardly avoid being heavily influenced in one way or another, through interest rate or exchange rate effects, by monetary policies of the relatively dominant German economy.

A complete loss of an independent U.S. monetary policy would not occur until a world currency is adopted—an unlikely event in this writer's opinion, looking at least several generations ahead. In the long, long meanwhile, we can hope that international economic discussions may become more effective. Perhaps evolving major currency areas, as they become stronger and more equal, will become more aware of the benefits to all of reasonable compromise on resolving payments imbalances among them. A utopian thought, but one can only hope.

Note

1   The Fed's view of its role as supervisor of a bank holding company is described in the following quote from its booklet, *Purposes and Functions of the Federal Reserve System*, published by the Board of Governors in June 2005 (the latest edition available as of this writing): "The Federal Reserve's role as the supervisor of a bank holding company or a financial holding company is to review and assess the consolidated organization's operations, risk-management systems, and capital adequacy to ensure that the holding company and its nonbank subsidiaries do not threaten the viability of the company's depository institutions. In this role, the Federal Reserve serves as the "umbrella supervisor" of the consolidated organization. In fulfilling this role, the Federal Reserve relies to the fullest extent possible on information and analysis provided by the appropriate supervisory authority of the company's bank, securities, or insurance subsidiaries." (p. 65)

7

THE FED'S TWO GREAT POSTWAR CRISES

In what ways are the two great postwar crises similar?

On the face of it, they are hardly similar at all. The first, the great inflation crisis encompassed the 1970s and the first part of the 1980s. It involved circumstances where market structure, surrounding sociopolitical conditions, and conservative Fed leadership worked against an aggressive anti-inflation policy; and then, as circumstances changed and under new Fed leadership, a daring monetary policy initiative was adopted convincingly to end it.

The second, the great credit crisis showed overt early signs in the latter part of 2007, culminated in late 2008 and early 2009, and its aftermath of frustratingly slow economic growth is still with us at the beginning of 2013. It involved problems that arose in part because regulatory and monetary policy officials did not recognize its potential depth. Then it required policy adaptations that went well beyond the Fed's usual instruments and experience to deal with it.

Nonetheless, while involving different subjects and different overall financial and social environments, both crises are similar in that their resolutions caused the Fed to stretch policy implementation into territory well beyond its norm (into innovative *terra incognita*), which was required in part by the nature of the crises and in part by an urgent need to regain its market and institutional credibility that had most unfortunately been lost. Also, while the heights of the crisis were relatively brief, they both ultimately involved surprisingly sustained periods of time.

It could stretch to around 15 years for the inflation crisis from the initial inflationary uptick in the late 1960s through to the early 1980s when inflation began to be well controlled. The great credit crisis remained an economic influence for about five years, including the associated weak economic recovery through 2012. It could easily be stretched another ten years or so back if its seeds in the financial attitudes and policy behavior during the buildup toward and in the aftermath of the stock market crash of 2000 were included.

They are the long, defining moments of the postwar Fed and have been the focus of many intense public discussions of the institution's role.[1]

How did the Fed become involved in the great inflation's onset?

The great inflation evolved slowly and then later burst forth. Initially, it crept up as military spending expanded in the course of the Vietnam War. The Fed did not keep inflation as fully under control as it should have at the time. This seemed to occur in part because federal budgetary estimates underestimated the full extent of the military buildup, so that its impacts on real GDP were not fully realized by policymakers. The public began to become more sensitized to aggregate price behavior and inflation expectations appeared to pick up by the early 1970s, following the long postwar period of relatively low, stable inflationary conditions.

Subsequently, the oil price shocks, noted in the preceding chapter, precipitated the shift of what had been a moderate inflation into, in the end, a great one in size and duration. The shocks were transnational, strongly raising inflationary pressures generally in industrialized, oil-dependent countries. And the Fed, under Chairman Burns, found itself in an unexpected situation that was very hard to control.

The Fed's monetary policy and its implementation were, as it turned out, not adequate to keep its already eroding anti-inflation credibility from becoming more of a market factor. It had announced money supply objectives as a token of its anti-inflation determination—to assure the public and markets that too much money would no longer chase too few goods. But in practice, it became apparent that the Fed was paying little attention to these targets. For instance, the institution forgave overshoots of its announced targets and reset them at higher levels. One of the governors of the day, Henry Wallich, publicly decried what he popularized as "base drift."

With inflation remaining quite high by earlier postwar standards, inflation expectations in financial, labor, and product markets became more pervasive. Domestic confidence in the value of the dollar deteriorated; labor costs and prices came under considerable upward pressure. Confidence in the dollar on foreign exchange markets also weakened. The second oil price shock, something of a crowning blow, came late in the 1970s during Chairman Miller's brief period in office.

How did the Fed control inflation and regain credibility?

It became apparent that forceful action was required to restore the Fed's credibility in the markets and with the public before a dire situation turned into one that risked a breakdown in domestic and worldwide confidence in the dollar. Shortly after taking office, Chairman Volcker proposed, and, in late 1979, the FOMC initiated a paradigm shift in how monetary policy was implemented. It was designed to impress deeply skeptical markets with the Fed's strong and definite intention finally to curb inflation and bring it down.

Rather than continue with the usual approach of implementing policy through step-by-step changes in money market conditions, which had been too cautious to adequately restrain the inflationary buildup, the FOMC decided to directly control the money stock in the hands of the public. It set annual money supply targets. But to make it more convincing that the targets would be attained, it instructed the account manager to aim his operations at providing the amount of aggregate reserves directly subject to his control (the nonborrowed reserves provided by open market operations) as calculated to keep money supply growth on its targeted anti-inflation path.

In the past, the amount of nonborrowed reserves provided by the manager would depend on the FOMC's decision about its strategic operating objective for the funds rate, as explained in chapter 4. But at the height of Volcker's anti-inflation battle, the situation was reversed. The funds rate (within a wide range) would depend on the FOMC's decision about the money supply objective and the implied amount of reserves to be provided by the manager.

Volcker called this approach "practical monetarism." It was new and strange to markets, far different from how the Fed had previously conducted policy in the postwar period or would again in the future, after inflation was under control, when an indicator of money market conditions (mainly the federal funds rate) returned as the principal operating objective of policy. Initially, markets remained cynical about the new approach.

To try to smooth the way and help accelerate efforts to restore the Fed's anti-inflation credibility and reduce inflation expectations, Volcker went around the country saying that the Fed would stick to it. That was done not only to convince markets of the Fed's determination, but also, and perhaps more crucially, business and labor, because lower domestic price and labor cost pressures would reduce inflationary expectations and hasten the return to a more stable economic situation. The policy did succeed in the end, but the process was a bit harrowing.

After a short recession and subsequent recovery associated with President Carter's imposition and retraction of his brief preelection price control program, the Fed's anti-inflation initiative began clearly to take hold. Inflation was cut by about two-thirds, to the neighborhood of 3% to 4% at an annual rate after a few years, but at the cost of a fairly severe recession. The unemployment rate peaked at about 10.5%, and the related recession covered some 16 months.[2] However, the recovery was quite rapid, averaging almost 7.75% at an annual rate year over its first six quarters before falling back to a rate much closer to the country's long-run potential.

All in all, the successful aftermath of the Volcker initiative owed much to the circumstances in which it took place. Business and consumers were well primed to resume spending after a decade or so of modest growth on balance and market-shaking shocks and uncertainties. Their optimism was fueled by the better tone emerging in the stock market following nearly 15 years of often substantial ups and downs but little net change on average.

In general, given macro-economic problems of the previous decade, the abatement of inflation was greeted with a sigh of relief. Moreover, on the policy front, there seemed to be growing understanding—not only here but in many major countries abroad—that a relatively low and stable inflation rate would also pave the way for more consistent growth.

After the successful battle against inflation, the economic and financial environment for monetary policy became much more stable. Monetary policy had, so it came to seem, entered a new period of fairly smooth sailing.

What again destabilized the economic and financial background for Fed policy?

Following the recession that marked the end of the great inflation, about 20 years of both generally satisfactory economic growth and contained inflation would pass before attainment of the Fed's duel economic mandate once again began to appear problematic. The economic and financial environment for policy became highly unstable. But this time, conflicts between the Fed's fundamental objectives of keeping inflation contained while also sustaining adequate economic growth did not turn out to be at issue.

Rather, fulfilling its dual mandate in practice was, for a time, set aside because the Fed, beginning most notably in 2008, had to take on its other principal role, that of ensuring markets remained functional and a deep depression averted. The persistent inflationary attitudes that had dominated market culture and complicated policy in the 1970s had been replaced, after the long period of stability, by a culture in which speculative attitudes and undue reliance on credit financing by market participants and among the public were fostering market bubbles, in both equity and mortgage markets. Such developments created complications for Fed policy every bit as difficult, and in the end more so, as the problems inherent in the earlier inflation years.

How did the Fed become involved in the great credit crisis?

As related earlier, the first fairly evident market manifestation of the great credit crisis seemed to occur in 2007, when the longer end of the normally very efficient and smoothly functioning interbank federal funds market began faltering. The Fed, in response, by year-end had been forced to implement a special program of term borrowing at its discount window.

But going back somewhat further, the implosion of the speculatively driven stock market bubble around the beginning of the new century and the threatening, though fairly brief, eight-month recession that followed, seemed to herald—in reality revealed—a new, less stable background environment for monetary policy. In fact, for a time after the stock market crash, the Fed conducted a prolonged highly easy monetary policy, in part to guard against the small but dangerous risk of falling into disinflation.

Unfortunately, as discussed before, a feature of Greenspan's easy money policy in the early years of the new century that seemed to assure low rates for a long period might have unwittingly reinforced this attitudinal shift. It seemed to reduce the risk to leverage—of borrowing short to invest long. It was probably more significant, or more prone to over interpretation, because it was taking place within a receptive broad cultural shift that was influencing the behavior of the populace, markets, and regulators.

As the first decade of the new century progressed, individuals were leveraging themselves into quite expensive homes relative to their income. Financial institutions also seemed to take on more risk by increasing the degree of leverage, borrowing more to hold profitable assets. In that context, institutions also became involved in a complex link of borrowing and lending among themselves here and abroad. Risk may have been dispersed, but the financial system itself, highly leveraged and interlinked as it was, became subject to more systemic risk.

Markets had come to be viewed as highly liquid, capable of diluting risk by shifting and sharing it through more extensive use of derivative instruments, such as options and futures contracts, and through newly developed credit default swaps and complex collateral debt obligations marketed by banks and other financial institutions. Unfortunately, as the new century progressed, distinctions between hedging, pure speculation, and marketing and holding investments became increasingly hazy and the risk parameters often seemed unclear even to allegedly sophisticated investors.

As financial markets became more complex and competitively interactive, the risks to the financial system as a whole were tending to expand as problems in one area or sector had more potential to affect others. It was believed by a number of powerful officials that markets would resolve their own problems should they arise—as they often (but not always) did.

Ultimately, it appeared that banking and other financial regulators both here and abroad were too relaxed in face of the huge technological innovations in finance and the change in attitudes toward credit. They seemed enmeshed, as were politicians, in the attitudes and culture of the times. For 20 years or so, regulators in the United States had focused for the most part on deregulation to make banks and other financial institutions more competitive and more suited to the modern financial world. While our entrepreneurial and risk-taking culture over time provides the dynamism behind the country's economic growth, the fabric of our financial system by the early part of the twenty-first century was being stretched toward a breaking point.

That fabric was noticeably beginning to fray further in the course of 2008 when a serious crisis in a relatively small subprime sector of the mortgage market spread widely and with unexpected intensity through other markets. In the spring, the Fed, with the support of the U.S. Treasury, made an emergency loan to support the purchase by a member bank of a troubled securities firm, Bear Stearns. The unstable market situation subsequently settled down a bit, though far from abated, even as the Fed also undertook a few other measures to assure adequate liquidity, including a continued easing of the funds rate from its earlier cyclical high.

By September of that year, however, the underlying instability was increasingly revealed. The knock-on effect from overlapping linkages and contagion among markets in the contemporary world, exacerbated in intensity by high leverage throughout, was beginning seriously to threaten the whole financial fabric. The house of cards, to shift metaphors, seemed more and more likely to tumble. And to shift yet again—what some have termed a "perfect storm" was in the works.

In that environment, the Fed refused to lend emergency funds to another securities firm, the venerable Lehman Brothers, which was faced with bankruptcy. There has been much discussion of why it did not, in view of the Bear Stearns precedent. A number of explanations can be offered: collateral was deemed inadequate; fears of reinforcing a moral hazard precedent had become stronger; it was not realized how close the market was to complete collapse; the Treasury did not give its support. This author would place most emphasis on the last two, although that is one man's opinion. In any event, within several hours, the Fed, with Treasury support, was forced by dangerously weakening market circumstances to make a large emergency loan to the insurance giant, AIG, to avert a total credit market collapse.

The stock market had been declining on balance for some time, much as it normally does in anticipation of a recession, but in that environment, it shifted gears into a decline that threatened a free fall. It was spurred on by contentious and delayed negotiations with and within the Congress for legislation needed by the Treasury to help it alleviate the crisis. Authority was needed, for example, to remove, at a price, the balance sheet burden of bad and deteriorating securities from market institutions, or otherwise strengthen their weakening capital positions. The process was unconscionably in a state of disarray and delay, partly because the Treasury (and apparently the Fed) showed no evidence of any contingency planning that might provide a useful guidepost, and mainly because the Congress was closely divided in an election period. Legislation was finally passed, though not without further damaging public confidence in the government's ability to manage crises and also itself.

What actions did the Fed take to help contain the crisis?

It was around this time that the Fed, out of sheer necessity, transformed itself from a conventional central bank whose balance sheet had for the postwar period remained relatively limited in size as needed for focusing almost entirely on its monetary policy objectives. Instead, it became a central bank whose balance sheet was greatly enlarged in order to provide the enormous liquidity needed by financial institutions to keep credit markets from collapsing (see especially the Fed balance sheets shown in Appendix A-2 as they contrast with those in Appendix A-1). It was as if the Fed was forced to become a key player in the business of finance, in addition to its central banking role of influencing national market conditions through its monetary policy instruments.

The total assets held by the Fed rose very quickly, as only a central bank with its unlimited power to create credit can do, more than doubling in short order from a not too far from normal $940 billion in mid-September 2008 just before the credit crisis began to a stratospheric $2.3 trillion in mid-December 2008. Practically all the increase in additional credit was employed in crisis-related credit extensions, and certain others, most of which had to be newly developed once the crisis had become more intense.

The Fed's credit was needed to keep markets functioning as private lenders became more and more stressed and backed away. This newly created liquidity gradually calmed the situation; markets began to seem self-sustainable, and the use of the Fed's crisis-related facilities began ebbing in the spring of 2009. In a limited sense, the credit crisis had been resolved—thanks also, of course, to the Treasury's large infusions of capital and funding to major banking and other institutions—but economic growth in its aftermath would prove to be long and agonizingly slow. In fact, the aftermath should be considered a lingering part of the crisis.

How did the Fed contribute to the recovery?

While the Fed could put money markets back on their feet by flooding them with liquidity, it was much more difficult to make consumers and businesses want to spend and institutions to lend. Public confidence was severely damaged by the financial collapse and the apparent unpreparedness of officialdom. A very large drop in real GDP in the fourth quarter of 2008 immediately after the Lehman debacle, by almost 9% at an annual rate, followed by further substantial weakness early in the next year was a clear economic signal of a huge loss in confidence. The cyclical downturn that had already been under way was greatly intensified.

Based on the business cycle reference dates published by the National Bureau of Economic Research, the credit crisis recession lasted 18 months, from the end of 2007 to mid-2009, only a little longer than the anti-inflation recession under Volcker, but it was a steeper one. However, the main difference between the two economic cycles was the pace of recovery.

The recovery from the credit-crisis-induced recession was clearly disappointing. Economic growth over the first year and a half after the cyclical trough—often a period of good-sized initial growth impelled by pent-up demands—averaged only about a subpar 2.5% at an annual rate over the first year and a half of recovery, and the unemployment rate barely edged down from its peak of just below 10% on average. Though it showed some decline subsequently, it still remained unacceptably high for the next two years as real economic growth through 2012 actually fell off on average from its sluggish pace in the early phase of the recovery period.

By the time the credit crisis came under control the Fed had already reduced the funds rate to its zero lower bound, and nothing further could be done to ease money market conditions. Moreover, much of the huge increase in liquidity provided by the Fed to keep the credit crisis from worsening was, as noted before, simply not used for spending or lending. As often has occurred over history in the wake of major crises, the public and financial institutions pulled back into a protective shell for a long period afterward.

For instance, a large part of the bank reserves created by the massive rise in Fed credit since the crisis began was kept idle as excess reserves in the hands of banks. They rose sharply from normal postwar levels of a just a few hundred million dollars to the neighborhood of $1.5 trillion dollars during 2012. The Fed, as earlier noted, has been paying banks one-quarter of a percent on these balances (more than what was being earned by idle cash held by most individuals), which can seem in the circumstances of a slow economic recovery a debatable, unearned reward—perhaps it would have been better to have desisted and by implication, provided a signal to banks that more productive use of those reserves should be more seriously contemplated.

In any event, in the absence of an adequate domestic fiscal stimulus and with foreign economies and U.S. export markets having their own problems, the Fed necessarily turned, as already explained, to massive purchases of longer-term securities to help stimulate the economy. These operations probably helped to accelerate healing in mortgage markets and to improve the financing environment in corporate bond markets.

For a while, they were financed by funds released through the continued drop in the Fed's short-term assets related particularly to the credit crisis, but after a time, they were funded by newly created bank reserves and Fed credit. This added even further to the size of the Fed's balance sheet. By of the beginning of 2013, it totaled almost $3 trillion, with 90% held in outright holdings of longer-term government and guaranteed mortgage-related securities.

Still, despite massive quantitative easing and acquisitions of longer-term government instruments, the economy remains mired in subpar growth rates as of this writing, almost three and a half years after the cyclical trough—additional evidence of the inherent limitations of monetary policy for stimulating growth when public confidence is at a low ebb and neither fiscal policy nor growth abroad are adequately supportive.

What lessons can be learned from the Fed's management of the two great postwar crises?

The Fed, in the end, effectively employed the powers available to it to contain the crises. But it should be recognized that the institution's freedom of action and effectiveness is influenced and limited not only by the reach of its powers but also by a whole host of factors outside its control. In short, the Fed is one important agent influencing the nation's credit markets and economy, but it functions within an economy and society susceptible to many other powerful influences—social, political, and economic—that strongly bear on financial and economic conditions.

For instance, the Fed's capability to control inflation is comparatively straightforward. It can just hold back on the aggregate amount of money and credit in the markets through its usual monetary policy instruments. Yet, in doing so, it has to take account of repercussions on other aspects of the economy and particularly implications for its employment objective.

The inflation crisis built over a number of years. Perhaps the Fed could have acted more forcefully earlier than it did. But the more rigid financial structure of the 1970s suggested the risk of a very serious recession at the time. The political and social conditions of the period indicated that the Fed had little public support for strong action. So it chose the cautious approach of containing rather than more actively forcing down the inflation rate. A more aggressive chairman might have spurred the FOMC to push harder and made a better public case for doing so. In any event, such a person would not have been appointed, given the spirit of the times.

Once the problems of inflation had lasted long enough and public patience with the related disturbances ended (such as long gas lines, the continuing uncertainties of adjusting to the push and pull of rising labor costs and prices), a new more aggressive chairman could find sufficient support to bring the inflation to a halt. Political resistance was eased as the evolution of money market funds permitted small savers to earn higher interest rates from tight money policies than was formerly available to them. The ability of savers to earn high interest as the Fed tightened monetary policy tended to balance the political playing field, which had formerly seemed tilted in favor of borrowers like small businesses, farmers, and homeowners.

When a new chairman sensed the moment had come where forceful action had become socially and politically more acceptable, and with the economic and financial conditions particularly compelling, the Fed could take a bold initiative that ended the inflation crisis more effectively than many might have expected. It was not without pain, but it was followed by so rapid an economic recovery that the pain was soon forgotten. One element in the policy's success was the famous incident in which President Reagan broke the air traffic controller's strike, providing a contagion effect that may have helped lower wage-cost pressures more broadly, smoothing the way for reasonable price stability to emerge more quickly out of the recession.

The credit crisis proved much harder to handle. Inflation can easily be seen. The problem becomes how quickly to act and with what intensity. Credit problems sufficient to build into a crisis are hard to see or anticipate as they develop. Credit issues are something like a daily fact of life in markets and in the life of regulators. But it is rare when they somehow coalesce into a threatening whole.

That, of course, is why the Fed should place more emphasis on evaluation of systemic market developments and to bring regulatory issues more to the fore in the monetary policy process. But in the regulatory area, the Fed does not have, as already stressed, the same unique authority as it does for monetary policy. It is shared with many other regulators and, above all, the U.S. Treasury.

The experience of the Fed in resolving the credit crisis does raise the question of how large a role the Fed should play compared with other governmental entities. It seems clear that the government, as it did, should take on responsibility for emergency-type lending to allay a crisis, especially the riskier loans (or capital injections) deemed necessary to avert a systemic market collapse and an economic depression. This seems properly a matter of strong national interest to be settled in the ongoing political process.

Another issue raised by the Fed's actions in the credit crisis revolves around the liquidity of its balance sheet. While it is very easy for the Fed to create credit, the Fed needs readily saleable assets on hand to reduce credit as quickly as might be needed for, say, anti-inflationary purposes—these traditionally being Treasury bills and other government securities with very short remaining maturities. The greatly enlarged and less liquid balance sheet that the Fed has been left with following the crisis could complicate problems for it when the economy returns closer to normal, and it becomes necessary to mop up the excess liquidity created during the credit crisis and its troublesome aftermath. The Fed probably now has the instruments to do so—including the newly available term deposits that can be placed at the Fed, as well as extensive continued use by the open market desk of reverse repurchase agreements. Still, the process, given its magnitude, could be testingly complex and unpredictable.

As a general point, though, the more the Federal government directly shares in ameliorating the financial risks in resolving a major crisis and in moderating the sluggish economic recovery that may well ensue, the less will the Fed's balance sheet suffer potentially debilitating distortions that may make it more difficult to conduct monetary policy once the crisis passes. The government did in fact take on a major part of the longer-run financial risks in the recent crisis. But it did not do its part, via a more proactive fiscal policy, in encouraging recovery from such a confidence-shaking major crisis.

Nonetheless, thus far confidence in the Fed's ability, once normal times loom, to overcome its extraordinary balance sheet acrobatics during the crisis and its aftermath has been reasonably well-maintained. This can be seen in the dollar's relatively strong performance on exchange markets and in the stability of domestic inflation expectations. As to the future, we will find out.

Notes

1   For a detailed discussion of the Fed's monetary policy activities during the periods covering the two crises see Stephen

H. Axilrod, *Inside the Fed: Monetary Policy and Its Management, Martin through Greenspan to Bernanke.* Rev. ed. (Cambridge, MA: MIT Press, 2011), especially the four chapters on Burns, Volcker, Greenspan, and Bernanke.

2   See announcement of business cycle turning points from the NBER on its website: nber.org/cycles.html.

8

CONCLUSION

What major challenges face the Fed as an organization in the future?

Judged from today's conditions, I would mention three.

First, the Fed needs somehow to bring regulatory issues more to the fore in considering its monetary policy. It seems to be working in that direction. That will be greatly helped when the president actually nominates a governor to become vice chairman for supervision, the position added in the DFA.

As earlier noted, the position has not yet been filled—left vacant since President Obama signed the DFA that created it into law in July 2010, about two and a half years ago from the time of this writing. While a governor can be designated by the chairman of the Board to perform the tasks, the position will evoke more authority and raise the profile of regulation within the Fed when held by a person who is sustained and perhaps even galvanized by the approval of both the President and the Senate for that particular task.

Nonetheless, the Fed's role and flexibility in better combining regulatory issues and monetary decisions will remain complicated by the wide dispersion of regulatory authority in the country—not to mention the long process still ahead for fully implementing the diverse provisions of the DFA, with the inevitable jockeying for bureaucratic authority and power that entails.

Fortunately, regulatory conditions and the overall stability of financial markets are likely to be seriously at cross-purposes with monetary policy rather infrequently. But when that happens, markets can then be subject to disruptions and crises so far beyond the norm that they are politically and socially destabilizing for the country. Against that background, the challenge for the Fed is to assure itself more regularly and more intensely than has been its wont in the past about the stability of the macro-financial system.

That could well require, among other things, something like a regular Fed assessment of the macro-financial system similar to its regular semiannual report on macro-economic developments and monetary policy required by the Congress (in addition to its newly required biennial report on its own supervisory activities).

Second, it behooves the Fed to continue with its efforts to regain the institutional credibility with the public and the Congress that was severely shaken by the credit crisis. It had been thrown into so much doubt that even the Fed's viability as an independent institution or, perhaps more practically, as an institution that could pursue its independent powers as effectively as desired seemed in question.

Some progress has been made to date I believe, but the institution's credibility will again be tested once the economic after-effects attributable purely to the psychological damage from the crisis are behind us (they probably are by now). The FOMC will then have to begin making the very difficult decisions and choices implicit in its dual mandate for monetary policy. For instance, how much inflation will the nation need or tolerate for a potential economic recovery to be strong enough to revive the country's sense of well-being? Or, if recovery falters much longer, how much more willing would the Fed and its principal officials feel about speaking even more plainly about the limits of monetary policy compared with other governmental policies in face of economic weakness?

If, or to be more historically accurate, when the economy once again becomes more cyclically volatile, the substance of the Fed's more open communication policies—in general a plus to its credibility—might be in need of fine-tuning. There seems no doubt that the prompt announcements about the specifics of current policy have been and will remain important for policy implementation and credibility. But only time will tell whether indications of future policy intent and the quarterly forecasts of key economic developments will need further tinkering, in one way or another, if they are to help bolster the Fed's reputation over the long run. However that may be, the Fed's institutional stature will depend, as usual, almost wholly on how the economy performs and on how well inflation is contained.

Nonetheless, since economic volatility will remain a fact of life the Fed's stature will also depend in some degree on how the public judges whether it is performing as well as it can in the face of all the economic, political, social, and worldwide circumstances that are well beyond its control. That impression will depend importantly on the ability of its chairman, the only official of the Fed who can authoritatively represent the institution, to communicate with the public and markets in a way that appears both empathetic and convincing. It may also depend on the Fed's ability to manage itself (and the president to use his appointive powers) to ensure that the institution is broadly governed and run consistent with the need to bring sound judgment from all walks of life into the sophisticated economic but also very practical issues it necessarily deals with.

To be convincing, a chairman's views need to be expressed with a popular touch that does not turn off the 99.7% or so of the people who find economics to be arcane and even something of a "dismal science"—a label often and rather unfairly attached to the field.[1] Obviously, that is a combination of virtues not easy to find in one person, whether trained as an economist, as have been four of the past five chairmen of the postwar period, or not.

Third, though less pressing a challenge than the previous two, would be an effort to intensify thinking about structural and operational adaptations as the startling, technologically driven innovations of recent decades continue. The structure of the Federal Reserve System itself might appear increasingly outdated, as economies and financial markets of regions of the country become more and more interdependent and the operational role of regional banks appears less crucial.

However, it is very doubtful that the useful role of regional banks in carrying out payments, examinations, and lending functions, as well as giving the Fed and its national monetary policy a more human local presence, would ever fade away. Still, there are likely to be further changes in the distribution of economic and financial activity that could, at some point as technology bounds further and unpredictably forward, raise political questions about the distribution, number, and size of regional banks. Many of the underlying issues are already being taken into account, it would seem, as the Fed does its own administrative restructuring to keep in step with, if not in the forefront of, the radical changes in financial technology affecting the private markets with which it is inextricably interlinked. It would seem that more is in store, somewhere down the line.

How well has the Fed served the country?

This author's opinion is "fairly well." The inflation of the 1970s in the United States was on the moderate side of what was happening in many other developed countries at a time when inflation and inflation expectations were becoming something of a worldwide phenomenon, intensified by the oil price shocks of the period.[2]

And the great credit crisis with its associated deep recession in the second decade of the new century—a major and virtually unprecedented challenge for the Fed—has come to seem less unique in view of unfolding events in Europe and elsewhere. It is not too much of a stretch to find that something like a "buy and borrow now and worry later" syndrome infecting the culture of the period has afflicted other areas of the world as well.

The Fed, while not without a responsibility for the onset and depth of the crisis, has handled the recovery process as well as could be reasonably expected. It has done what it could. It has filled up the punch bowl just about to overflowing, but the party has so far been very quiet.

When it livens up, the Fed will have to begin the task of emptying the bowl. It will be a big task. Fortunately, the Fed's policy instruments are traditionally more effective on the restrictive than the expansive side. During the recovery from the crisis, more help from an expansionary fiscal policy would have made the party better. But the timing of fiscal policy, and the political and social factors influencing it, is another and rather sad story.

As to the Fed and monetary policy, looking back over the past 60 years or so, there is no doubt that mistakes were made. The inflation of the 1970s could have been more strongly resisted. In recent years, the stock market and housing bubbles might well have been pricked before they got so far out of hand. Still, in the end, the Fed successfully did what central banks were invented to do. It was quite responsive to its counter-cyclical obligations, it brought inflation under control, and it reliquified and helped regenerate a collapsing credit market.

Notes

1   It was first popularized in mid-nineteenth-century disputes in England during the early years of the economic "science's" founding.

2   The average annual rate of inflation of the CPI in the United States over the major inflationary period of 1973–1979 was 8.5%, according to statistics published by Organisation for Economic

Cooperation and Development (OECD). This was below the average of seven major OECD countries for the same period of 9.7%. This grouping included, in addition to the United States, Japan, Germany (West only at the time), France, the United Kingdom, Italy, and Canada. Only West Germany was lower, with a rate averaging 4.7%. It should be pointed out, however, that the U.S. inflation rate had moved somewhat above the average of those countries in 1979 and then in 1980, when it averaged a little under 12.5% for the two years, following the second oil price shock and just before the Fed's anti-inflation initiative began to take hold. Source: *Historical Statistics, 1960– 1990* (Paris: OECD, 1992), p.87.

Appendix A-1

Fed Balance Sheet Organized as Factors Affecting Reserve Balances (figures in billions of dollars; daily averages for week ending)

	I	II
	Sept. 27, 2006	Sept. 10, 2008
Total of factors supplying reserves (Assets)	876.6	940.3
Outright holdings of U.S. Treasury securities	768.9	479.8
Repurchase agreements	16.6	110.8
Regular discount window credit	.4	19.9
Crisis related credit extensions	0	179.4
Various other	90.6	150.5
Total of factors absorbing reserves (Liabilities)	876.6	940.3
Reverse repurchase agreements	28.4	42.7
Deposits at F.R. Banks other than reserve balances	11.6	12.3
Other liabilities and capital	36.2	42.5
Currency in circulation	790.8	834.6
Reserve balances with F.R. Banks	9.7	8.0
Addendum: Implied Monetary Base	800.5	842.6

Note: Appendix tables are based on figures in table 1 of the H.4.1 statistical releases published weekly by the Federal Board of Governors. Some items in the published accounts have been either renamed or grouped together for clarity in presentation in the context of this book. For instance, the loans termed primary, secondary, and seasonal credits have been grouped under the title "regular discount window credit." The term "Crisis related credit extensions" encompasses a variety of other loan programs for banks and other financial institutions designed to ease the crisis, such as term auction credit, commercial paper funding facility, money market mutual fund liquidity facility, broker dealer credit, and credit extended to individual financial institutions. Other credit crisis-related debt has also elevated regular discount window credit to a degree and also items shown as other in the balance sheet. Components may not add to total because of rounding. The addendum measure of the monetary base is the sum of the entries for "currency in circulation" and "reserve balances with F.R. Banks" on the liability side of the balance sheet.

Appendix A-2

Fed Balance Sheet Organized as Factors Affecting Reserve Balances (figures in billions of dollars; daily averages for week ending)

	III	IV
	Dec. 17, 2008	Jan. 9, 2013
Total of factors supplying reserves (Assets)	2,305.8	2,966.7
Outright security holdings, total	492.8	2,674.8
U.S Treasury	476.2	1,671.4
Federal agency	16.6	76.7
Mortgage-backed securities	0	926.7
Repurchase agreements	80.0	0
Regular discount window credit	88.4	.6
Crisis related credit extensions	951.4	2.9
Various other	693.2	289
Total of factors absorbing reserves (liabilities)	2,305.8	2,966.7
Reverse repurchase agreements	93.2	88.2
Deposits at F.R. Banks other than reserve balances	454.7	79.7
Other liabilities and capital	82.3	66.8
Currency in circulation	875.3	1,126.8
Reserve balances with F.R. Banks	800.3	1,505.9
Addendum: Implied Monetary Base	1,675.3	2,632.7

Note: See note to table in Appendix A-1.

INDEX

CPSIA information can be obtained
at www.ICGtesting.com
Printed in the USA
BVHW071525290323
661265BV00003B/14